Touring
NEW MEXICO
HOT SPRINGS

Help Us Keep This Guide Up to Date

Every effort has been made by the author and editors to make this guide as accurate and useful as possible. However, many things can change after a guide is published—trails are rerouted, regulations change, techniques evolve, facilities come under new management, etc.

We would love to hear from you concerning your experiences with this guide and how you feel it could be improved and kept up to date. While we may not be able to respond to all comments and suggestions, we'll take them to heart and we'll also make certain to share them with the author. Please send your comments and suggestions to the following address:

The Globe Pequot Press
Reader Response/Editorial Department
P.O. Box 480
Guilford, CT 06437

Or you may e-mail us at:

editorial@GlobePequot.com

Thanks for your input, and happy travels!

Touring
NEW MEXICO
HOT SPRINGS

By Matt Bischoff

FALCONGUIDE®

GUILFORD, CONNECTICUT
HELENA, MONTANA
AN IMPRINT OF THE GLOBE PEQUOT PRESS

A **FALCON** GUIDE ®

Cover photo: The Gila River below Melanie Hot Springs.

All photographs are by the author unless otherwise noted.

Library of Congress Cataloging-in-Publication Data

Bischoff, Matt C.
    Touring New Mexico hot springs / by Matt Bischoff.
        p. cm. —(A Falcon guide)
    ISBN-13: 978-0-7627-4109-0
    ISBN-10: 0-7627-1134-5
    1. Hot springs—New Mexico—Guidebooks. 2. New Mexico—Guidebooks.
I. Title. II. Series.
GB 1198.3.N6 B57 2001
551.2'3'09789—dc21   00-064645

 Text pages printed on recycled paper.

Manufactured in the United States of America
First Edition/Second Printing

CONTENTS

NORTHERN NEW MEXICO HOT SPRINGS

OVERVIEW MAP

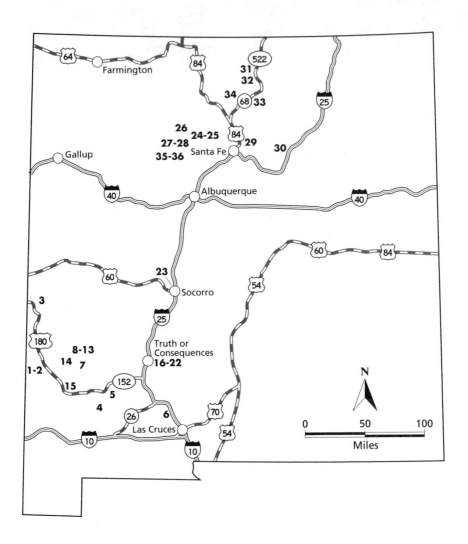

Map Legend

Interstate	00		Campground	▲
US Highway	00	000	Picnic Area	⌐
State or Other Principal Road	00	000	Peak	9,782 ft.
Forest Route	00	000	City	City or ◯ City
Interstate Highway	⟹		Cabin/Building	■
Paved Road	⟹		Gate	•—•
Gravel Road	⟹		Point of Interest	◻
Road Junction	□		Airport	✕
One-Way Road	One-Way		Cliffs	
Main Trail(s) /Route(s)			National Forest/ Park Boundary	
Parking Area	Ⓟ		Fence	
River/Creek			Barbed-wire Fence	–x–x–x–x–x–
Intermittent Stream				
Bridge			Map Orientation	N
Meadow/Marsh				
Spring			Scale	0 0.5 1
Dam	—			Miles

INTRODUCTION

HOT SPRINGS IN HISTORY

Hot springs have held a central place in numerous cultures throughout time. Prehistorically, hot springs were used for bathing and food preparation, and had spiritual meaning for many diverse groups. According to archaeological evidence, balneology, the use of natural mineral waters for the treatment of disease, has been practiced for more than 5,000 years. Hot springs have been used in religious rites and ceremonies in both Egypt and the Middle East for thousands of years.

Bath, England

According to English legend, Prince Bladud (who later became the father of King Lear) contracted leprosy at a young age and was banished from his father's kingdom. The prince was forced to eke out a living from herding swine, but the pigs themselves contracted his disease. As the legend goes, one day the pigs were wallowing in hot-spring water on the banks of a river and emerged miraculously cured of their disease. Noticing this, the young prince also bathed in the water and was healed. The story of this incredible cure spread rapidly, and the hot-spring waters became a popular place to visit. Today, we know the site as Bath, England.

Several centuries later, Roman soldiers visited the site and recuperated from their long campaigns in the hot-spring water. Word of the springs spread across the Roman Empire, and Bath quickly developed as a resort town. Through the centuries, people continued to believe in the curing abilities of the waters at Bath. The Royal Mineral Water Hospital, established at Bath in 1739 by the British Parliament, evolved into a therapeutic treatment center for a variety of ailments.

The Victorian era in Europe saw a great awakening of interest in spas and hot-spring waters. People were primarily interested in the medicinal benefits attributed to drinking the waters, although bathing was still an important activity. A visit to a spa became a fashionable pastime for Europe's wealthy, and centers of thermal waters that had earlier been used by the Romans were developed into elaborate resort-hotel complexes.

Hot Springs in America

The popularity of hot-spring resorts in Europe carried over to America. Berkeley Springs in West Virginia, one of the first popular spas in North America, was originally named Bath in honor of the spa in England. Like most hot springs in North America, Native Americans had used Berkeley Springs long before the arrival of Europeans. Various tribes used the springs as a kind of neutral ground, where peaceful meetings could be held. The British colonials also used the hot springs as meeting places, and continued to believe in their therapeutic value.

New hot springs were "discovered" as Americans began moving west, and by 1888 there were 8,843 springs recorded in the United States. Of these, 634 were spas and 223 were sources of commercial mineral water for consumption. The popularity of hot springs was particularly pronounced from the 1880s through the turn of the century. Natural hot-spring pools and ponds had been used therapeutically for years, but people in the Victorian age desired a more civilized way of bathing. Resorts and spas became the answer, allowing for private and controlled bathing in the medicinal waters. Because of the lower population and lack of governmental support, however, American resort springs never became as extensive as their European counterparts.

The heyday for the establishment of spas and resorts at hot springs in the United States occurred in the early twentieth century. Ruins at countless hot springs in the country attest to this boom time in commercial hot-spring bathing. These resorts generally promised that their hot-spring waters contained preventive and curative values. By this time, transportation had vastly improved in the West, particularly with the arrival of the railroad, allowing people to visit places that would have been inaccessible otherwise. The hot-spring resorts at Tonopah and Castle Springs, Arizona, were both products of this time.

The fashion waned by the outbreak of World War I, but by that time all the major thermal areas in the eastern United States had been developed. In the West, such development was much less extensive because of the lower population density. By the 1950s, the boom in hot-spring resorts had passed, and many closed down or were simply abandoned never to reopen. Today, an increased interest in hot springs has spurred the reuse of previously abandoned springs, with varying results.

Today there are an estimated 1,800 hot springs in the United States, the majority of which are located in the western portion of the country, only about 115 have been developed into extensive resorts or spas.

Hot Springs in New Mexico

"New Mexico, the Land of Enchantment." After visiting the springs in this book, you will be hard-pressed to disagree with this slogan. New Mexico is also a land of geographic extremes, from the low desert in the south to the pine-clad Rocky Mountains in the north. The hot springs also range across the state's geographic diversity. Primarily, however, they're concentrated in the southwestern and north-central portion of the state. Geothermal activity in these two areas is some of the richest in the country. Most of New Mexico's geothermal resources, unfortunately (or fortunately, depending upon your point of view), are privately owned and closed to the public. However, enough hot springs, warm springs, and hot wells are available for public use to make New Mexico a must-visit for any geothermal enthusiast. The natural beauty of the state, along with an amazing array of outdoor activities, make visiting the springs doubly rewarding. Most of New Mexico's hot springs are located in natural settings and remain undeveloped. In some cases, hot springs that had been commercially developed have reverted back to a more natural state.

You will be amazed not only by the hot springs themselves and by the scenic beauty of the state, but also by the fact that much of New Mexico's history is intricately connected to these hot water sources. Native New Mexicans used the waters for centuries prior to the arrival of Europeans. Often located along major travel routes, the springs became well known to Spanish, Mexican, and Anglo pioneers. Hot springs were often the only source of water in a dry landscape, making them extremely valuable. As settlement increased in the state, the springs became more popular, and some were commercialized. Included among the more lavish hot-spring resorts in New Mexico were Faywood, Montezuma, and Radium springs. Today, they are mere shadows of themselves. Perhaps you will prefer them in their simpler, sometimes more natural state.

THERAPEUTIC ASPECTS

The therapeutic benefits of hot-spring water continue to be touted in several countries such as Portugal, Japan, Germany, and Czech Republic, but the fad waned considerably in the United States early in this century. The practice of balneology is prevalent in Europe and Japan, although largely unknown in the United States. According to some theories, this is because the claims of balneology are subjected to scientific scrutiny by modern medicine, and people are less inclined to believe in the so-called therapeutic benefits without medical endorsement.

Along with the perceived benefits of hot-spring water in medical therapy, many people believed, and continue to believe in the value of drinking mineral waters. A variety of minerals are said to have beneficial values when consumed in certain doses. In the 1700s, in fact, this belief served as a motivation for the development of the science of chemistry. Physicians during that period believed in the medical efficacy of certain mineral-spring waters. Many pioneers in the field of chemistry got their start by attempting to reproduce the chemical composition of the water found in many of the hot springs. These studies were largely driven by the consumption of carbonated beverages and the desire to know the role gases played in these beverages. Today, following a long period of waning popularity, the bottled-water industry is growing rapidly. Many of these bottled waters come from hot-spring or mineral-spring locales.

GEOLOGY OF HOT SPRINGS

Much is known about the geological setting of hot springs, the surface manifestation of what geologists term *geothermal systems*. Many of these systems have been tapped for the generation of electricity, as they are a clean source of energy to replace fossil fuels. Surface hot springs can be no hotter than the boiling point at the earth's surface (100 degrees C, or 212 degrees F). Waters at depth, however, can reach temperatures as high as 400 degrees C, or 752 degrees F! Such super temperatures are possible because the boiling point is raised by the high hydrostatic pressure at great depth, and because of the water's nearness to subsurface molten rock (magma).

The earth's heat originates deep beneath the crust, through the decaying of natural radioactive elements such as uranium, thorium, and potassium. Hot springs generally occur where the earth's heat, in the form of hot or molten rock, exists at relatively shallow depths. Areas of recent or active volcanic activity are obvious locales. Although hot springs are abundant in these regions, the most prevalent and spectacular ones are on the sea floor, far from human view. These underwater springs occur along chains of active submarine volcanoes called *spreading centers*, which are the places where the earth's tectonic plates diverge. Hot springs can also occur in places where there is no obvious source for the heating of the water (far from volcanic areas, for example). These hot springs are formed from magma bodies at depth with no surface manifestation, or the water itself has come from great depths where there is abundant heat. The water is then forced to the surface by some unknown means.

Hot springs occur because of convection. Just as air above a radiator rises as it expands from being heated, water also rises as it is heated. Rocks are generally full of cracks and fractures, and these inevitably become filled with water as rainwater percolates downward to fill all the voids. This water is collected in the porous rocks and kept as groundwater (where well water comes from). In mountainous regions, downhill from where the water first entered the fractured rocks, groundwater sometimes emerges again as springs, forced to the surface through some impermeable barrier. These natural cold-water springs occur because of simple gravity flow, and differ from hot springs, which flow because of convective forcing.

The convective process that causes hot springs occurs when groundwater near a recently injected molten body becomes very hot, even boiling. This heated water (and associated steam) is less dense than the surrounding cold groundwater, so it rises toward the surface, typically along a fault (see diagram). As the heated water rises, cold groundwater instantaneously moves into the void around the magma to replace the rising water, and convection begins. The system functions like a coffee percolator. The heated water rises, mixing with overlying water as it ascends. Although the rising water loses some of its heat to the rocks it passes through, it eventually discharges at the surface as a hot spring. Water flow, temperatures, and the chemical composition of hot-spring waters often remain stable for long periods of time, despite year-to-year variation in rainfall. This suggests that the complex plumbing systems are very deep and large. Once such convection systems are set up, they can last for hundreds of years, as heat is slowly harvested from the magma, forcing it to cool and solidify.

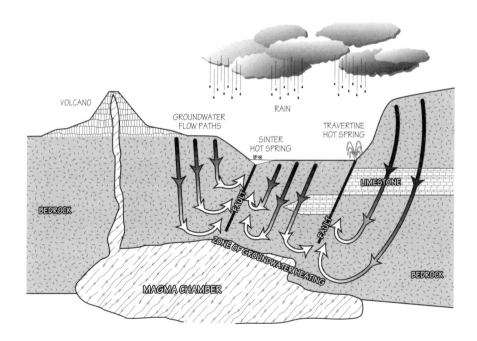

The chemical composition of the thermal waters is controlled by the rocks through which the waters pass. For example, some hot springs deposit calcium-carbonate-rich travertine around their orifices, such as Travertine Hot Springs in California or Mammoth Hot Springs in Yellowstone National Park. Waters of these springs leach and dissolve calcium carbonate from the limestone they pass through in the subsurface. When the thermal waters discharge at the surface, the water effervesces dissolved CO_2 gas in the same way soda pop effervesces when the bottle cap is removed. Loss of CO_2 results in the precipitation of calcium carbonate. Thus, hot springs with travertine are evidence of limestone below. In most volcanically active regions where limestone is not present, hot springs deposit siliceous sinter around their orifices. Sinter has an entirely different character than travertine and is relatively pure silica, the same composition as quartz and the most common constituent of igneous rocks. At room temperature, silica is almost insoluble, so we use it for glass. At the high temperatures at depth in the geothermal systems, however, silica is relatively soluble, so the thermal waters leach silica from the rocks. As the waters discharge, the silica becomes supersaturated as the spring cools, and the silica precipitates as sinter. These two different types of chemical deposits, sinter and travertine, tell us much about the subsurface geology through which the hot waters passed.

HOW TO USE THIS GUIDE

BOOK ORGANIZATION

New Mexico is a diverse state with a substantial number of hot and warm springs scattered throughout. Several of these hot water sources are actually hot wells—hot water that was discovered accidentally during drilling that is presently diverted for various uses. Many others are truly natural hot springs that are open to the public for bathing. Still others consist of warm springs that also provide bathing opportunities. During the summer months, these warm springs may be a more attractive alternative to their hotter counterparts. No matter which type you sample, New Mexico's geothermal resources are located in some of the most interesting country you can imagine. Take time to enjoy the state's splendor.

Like its predecessors, *Touring California and Nevada Hot Springs* and *Touring Arizona Hot Springs*, this guide does not pretend to be an exhaustive list of hot springs and hot-spring resorts in New Mexico. It is, instead, a guide to and description of some of the best hot springs in the state. Most of the springs you will find in this book are natural hot springs in natural settings, with just a few listings for developed hot-spring resorts. Additionally, this book is not strictly a guide to hot-spring soaking. Although many of the springs described offer wonderful bathing experiences, there are several worth visiting for other reasons. Several of these springs are in majestic settings, several more are in locations of historical or archaeological interest, and others offer features of geological interest. Before you visit any of them, please read the **"Precautions"** and **"Responsible Behavior"** sections below.

The book is organized geographically to allow for the greatest ease in traveling from one hot spring to the next. Following a general description of the spring, all the pertinent information you will need for a visit is provided. Subjects such as location, access, best time of year, helpful maps, and nearest services are listed. A detailed set of directions is given for each spring, followed by a more in-depth discussion and description of the spring itself.

The book is divided into two regions: Southern New Mexico and Northern New Mexico. In some cases, hot springs in one region may be closer to springs in another region than to those in its own. The lines between the regions are drawn arbitrarily, simply for the sake of organization. To find out what springs are in your vicinity, check the **Overview Map** of the state.

The book is also divided into subregions. These subregions are also arbitrary, although they are designed to give you a sense of place when visiting a hot spring or series of hot springs. Generally, these subregions also follow geographical lines. A short introduction pointing out some of the more salient features of the country is given for each region and subregion. In several places historical vignettes are also included to add some flavor to the region and put you far ahead of the casual tourist, who generally knows nothing about the country in which he or she is visiting.

USING THE DIRECTIONS AND MAPS IN THIS BOOK

Each set of directions is designed to be used in conjunction with the maps provided. These directions have all been field-checked and should get you to the springs with minimal confusion. The maps show the important features needed to reach the springs, but you'll need to pay close attention to the mileages described in the **"Finding the spring"** section of each entry. The maps do not always show all the features in the region; they're designed to be location aids, not replacements for a topographic map.

I recommend that you use a standard highway map and a United States Geological Survey (USGS) topographic map when visiting these springs. The quadrangle name of the recommended topographic map is listed under **"Map(s),"** prior to the **"Finding the spring"** section. For most springs that you can drive to, a 1:100,000-scale topographic map will generally suffice. When hiking is required, I strongly recommend obtaining the 1:24,000-scale map, which can be ordered directly from the USGS for $5 each (plus postage). They can also be found at many map stores and some specialty outdoor outlets. In several cases a USDA Forest Service map for a particular region is recommended. It is wise to contact the land management agency that has jurisdiction over the hot spring you plan to visit. Important information such as up-to-date road conditions, access, permit requirements, and weather can usually be obtained from these offices. Phone numbers for the Forest Service offices and other land management agencies are listed in the appendix.

PRECAUTIONS

Visiting hot springs carries with it certain risks and inherent dangers. Hot springs, after all, can contain scalding water. Pay attention to all directions and descriptions given in this book. Most dangers are pointed out to you, but not all can be anticipated. Do not, under any circumstance, get into water without first testing it in some way. You will usually be able to tell how hot a spring is just by going near the water. If you can feel the heat of the water from a few inches away, it's probably too hot. If the water is steaming, even on a warm day, it is also probably too hot. If the water appears to be fine, put a finger or hand in to test it. If your hand can't stay submerged without hurting, don't put your body in. More important, if you cannot see the bottom of a spring, don't get in. The water on the top of the spring may be fine, but deeper water may scald you. Also be careful around mud in hot springs because it can often hide extremely hot water. When in doubt, stay out.

Perhaps one of the most lethal dangers posed by certain hot springs is the presence of an amoeba, *Naegleria fowleri*. This amoeba enters human hosts via mucous membranes in the nose, causing an infection resembling meningitis. The infection is nearly always fatal. Do not put your head under the water or let the water enter your nose or mouth. This is generally wise behavior at any of the hot springs.

Since many of these springs are far from civilization, travel and safety precautions should be taken. Be sure your vehicle is in sound shape and able to make a long trip. Check on all engine fluids, including oil and coolant. Be sure that all the tires have the necessary pressure and that you have a spare (along with a jack and lug wrench), and know how to change a tire before you head out. By far the most common breakdown is a flat tire, and when driving on dirt roads, you will eventually get a flat. Rocks tend to get caught in the tire treads, occasionally puncturing the fabric of the tire. Always plan ahead when considering gasoline. Be sure you know how far you are going, what your gas mileage is, and where the next place that you can purchase gasoline is. The locations of the nearest services are given in each of the entries. If you plan on camping, make a checklist of the equipment you need before heading out. I recommend you take at least the following:

- ❑ spare tire, jack, lug wrench
- ❑ basic tool kit for the car (screwdrivers, wrenches, hammer, etc.)
- ❑ shelter of some kind (tent, etc.)
- ❑ extra clothing (including wet-weather gear)
- ❑ sleeping bag, insulating pad, and blankets
- ❑ food and water (more than you will need)
- ❑ stove or other means by which to cook food
- ❑ electrical tape
- ❑ rope
- ❑ shovel
- ❑ ax or small saw

- ❏ firewood
- ❏ candles
- ❏ matches
- ❏ flashlights
- ❏ extra batteries
- ❏ knife
- ❏ first-aid kit

Once you have packed all this gear, be sure to notify someone of your trip and when you expect to return. Even if you plan on being out for the day only, it's not a bad idea to take along most of this equipment, and you'll be glad you did if you do get stranded. Contact the land management agency that supervises the area into which you are heading. Ask about access, restrictions, and permit requirements. Be sure to keep a watch on the weather, and if storms threaten, stay off secondary dirt roads even if you have a four-wheel-drive vehicle. Avoid *all* dirt roads if you have a passenger vehicle. A road may not be wet when you depart, but may become impassable during and after a storm. When in the desert portions of New Mexico, be especially aware of thunderstorms and flash floods. Flash floods can occur even when it is not raining where you are. Desert washes can fill with no warning and become raging torrents. Do not, under any circumstances, make camp in a wash.

As many of the springs in this book require long hikes, be extra prepared when making these trips. Only those in sound physical shape should take the hikes, and some are recommended for experienced hikers only (Jordan, Turkey Creek). Mileage can be deceiving, since many of the routes described do not follow trails, or else require a fair amount of bushwhacking. Hiking up canyons, for example, will take you more than twice as long as hiking along a trail. This kind of hiking also wears you out faster and is harder on your joints. It is especially critical that you let someone know where you are going and when you are expected back. Do not attempt these trips alone, and be sure to bring plenty of water and food. The proper maps are also critical for these hiking trips.

RESPONSIBLE BEHAVIOR

Visiting hot springs carries with it a sort of unspoken etiquette. Since most of the hot springs described in this book are on public land, you will not be trespassing. However, a few of the springs are located on private land, and I recommend you do not trespass. In other cases, the landowners have allowed people to visit the springs on their property. In any case, respect private property. If there are "no trespassing" signs, obey them. This will prevent you from getting shot, and will help to keep numerous hot springs open to the public. Several of the springs are located on Indian reservations, and all posted rules should be obeyed. In several cases, overnight camping is not permitted and is usually posted as such. Campgrounds or other public lands that do not restrict camping can often be found nearby.

Two of the biggest problems faced by hot-spring enthusiasts are vandalism and trash. Most of the well-known hot springs have experienced some aspect of both. Graffiti, broken glass, trash, and off-road driving truly detract from the beauty these places hold. Be sure to pack out all trash, stay on established roads, and generally leave things as you found them (or better).

Many of the hot springs described in this book are visited quite often. Do not be surprised when you find people already at your hot-spring destination. People generally prefer privacy and will appreciate it if you let them finish their soak before you enjoy the water. This is especially true for families and couples. Others may enjoy your company, and a simple inquiry will let you know either way. Many locations offer several soaking opportunities, sometimes quite removed from each other.

Many people enjoy hot springs without bathing suits. For those hot springs in remote locations, this is generally the norm. Most public bathing facilities or those pools in public view generally require clothing, unless you have a private room. You will notice the prevalent trend at most springs. Again, obey any and all signs posted. Nudity has become prevalent at several springs, including Spence Hot Springs, Manby Hot Springs, Blackrock Hot Springs, Faywood Hot Springs, and the two San Francisco Hot Springs. If nudity offends you, you may not want to visit these springs, or you may wish to wait until you can have the site to yourself. Most of the resorts listed allow visitors to choose for themselves in their private rooms. These locations include the various hot-spring resorts in Truth or Consequences, along with Ten Thousand Waves.

Author's Favorites

A Hot Spring Close To The City: Ten Thousand Waves

If you are in the Santa Fe area, Ten Thousand Waves is a short distance away, and worth a visit. Few other hot springs are located this close to one of New Mexico's larger towns. Ten Thousand Waves, although a little expensive, provides virtually every type of hot-water experience you could ask for. There are numerous private tubs, communal tubs, and a broad array of massages and body treatments. Lodging is also available on the property.

For the Family: Montezuma Hot Springs

Located immediately off a paved road, Montezuma is set in a beautiful valley and is easy to reach. Families do not need to worry about nudity at Montezuma, since bathing suits are required for all bathers. The hot springs are surrounded by a fascinating set of ruins with an interesting history. Because there are several pools, families should not have too much difficulty finding a bathing spot. Do be careful, however, as some of the pools can be rather hot.

A Remote Experience: Turkey Creek Hot Springs

If you desire a challenge, both physically and mentally, Turkey Creek is your place. Requiring an 8-mile round-trip hike to visit, Turkey Creek Hot Springs is one of the more remote springs in the book. Although others require more hiking to reach, Turkey Creek is not located along a trail, and it can be tricky to find. The last few miles of the hike can be difficult, as you thread your way up the Turkey Creek Canyon. Once you finally reach the spring, however, you will be richly rewarded. Consisting of numerous seeps of hot and warm water, several bathing opportunities await you. Come prepared!

SOUTHERN NEW MEXICO
HOT SPRINGS

SAN FRANCISCO RIVER AREA

Along the San Francisco River in western New Mexico, there's a series of hot springs accessible only by foot. Known collectively as the San Francisco Hot Springs, they have been referred to by various names. Previously, Upper San Francisco Hot Springs was actually downstream of Lower San Francisco Hot Springs. To reduce confusion, I have referred to the upstream one as San Francisco Hot Spring, and the downstream one as Bubbles, which it is sometimes called. Access to these springs used to be along a USDA Forest Service road and a short hike along the river. This route crossed private property, however, and following many complaints, it was closed to the public. The Forest Service opened an alternate route to the south of the old road, which requires a slightly longer hike. For further information and the latest access issues, contact the Gila National Forest's Glenwood Ranger Station at 505-539-2481.

The other hot spring in the area, Frisco Box, also requires a hike. Because this is a much more vigorous hike than the previous two, Frisco Box receives much less visitation. Unfortunately, access issues have been a problem here, too. The previous route, which had been used for years, was closed a few years ago by landowners tired of disrespectful people. The Forest Service opened another route that avoided the private property but made it a much longer hike. The trip is well worth it, however, because the surrounding countryside is magnificent. Frisco Box Hot Springs is at a higher elevation than the other springs and therefore can only be visited during the warmer months. For up-to-date access information, as well as trail conditions and weather, be sure to call the Gila National Forest's Luna Ranger District at 505-533-6232.

1

Bubbles Hot Springs

General description: A natural pool of hot water alongside the San Francisco River that was formed by the scouring action of the river.

Location: Western New Mexico, southwest of the small towns of Glenwood and Pleasanton.

Primitive/developed: Primitive. There is no need to improve the pool for bathing.

Best time of year: Spring, summer, and fall. During winter roads can be too wet, and the river can be too high to cross.

Restrictions: The hot springs themselves are on national forest property. However, private property is nearby. Several areas are off-limits to vehicle access and camping. Be sure to obey all signs.

Access: The hot spring are accessible via a short drive down dirt road off U.S. Highway 180, followed by a hike of about 1 mile. You'll have to cross the river three times. The road is usually easily passable to most vehicles, but it can become impassable when wet.

Water temperature: The springs feeding the pool are about 105 degrees F; the pool is a few degrees cooler.

Nearby attractions: San Francisco Hot Springs, Mogollon.

Services: Gas, food, and lodging can be found in Glenwood, about 5 miles to the northeast.

Camping: Camping is not permitted at the hot spring themselves. Undeveloped camping is permitted 0.25 mile farther south along the river. There are also several USDA Forest Service campgrounds north along US 180.

Maps: USGS Dillon Mountain, New Mexico quadrangle (1:24,000 scale).

Finding the spring: From the small town of Pleasanton, travel south on US 180 for about 2 miles. Keep an eye out with a pair of binoculars for a Forest Service sign. A narrow gravel road is on your right immediately past this sign. If driving north on US 180, look for a similar sign on the left side of the road after crossing a bridge. This used to be the access route to the springs. Now, however, property owners have restricted access, and you must drive another 2 miles south on US 180 (south of the bridge over Dugway Wash) to an unsigned dirt road on the west side of the highway. You'll have to open a cattle gate; be sure to close it after driving through. Drive about 1 mile along this road, heading for a corral (stay right at a Y intersection). Park near the corral and look for a small trail to the west. Take the trail for about 1.25 miles down to the river. The last part of the trail is rather steep, so be careful. The trail will

Bubbles Hot Springs
San Francisco Hot Springs

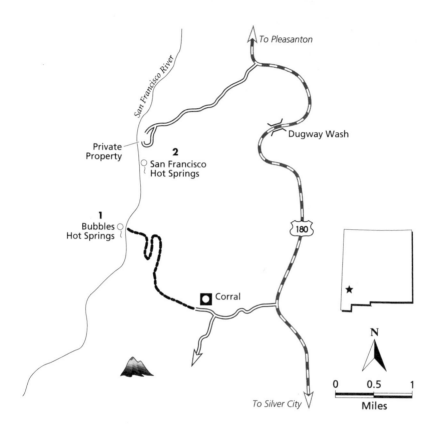

take you directly to Bubbles Hot Springs. To reach San Francisco Hot Springs, head north (upstream) along the river for about half a mile. The springs are located on the east side of the river, and are hard to miss. To reach the springs requires at least two crossings of the river. Do not attempt the crossings during high water levels.

The hot springs: Apparently, a large flood along the San Francisco River scoured out a portion of the cliffside adjacent to the river, uncovering several hot springs. At the same time, the flood deposited a sandbank in front of the hot springs, forming a kind of dam for the water. The pool remains today, replenished by the hot-spring water that bubbles up from the bottom and overflows back into the river. The pool is large (measuring about 50 x 100 feet) and several feet deep. The bottom is sandy. Located underneath the cliff, the pool is also under constant shade.

Bubbles Hot Springs provides a far better bathing opportunity than San Francisco Hot Springs. The pool here is much larger, more secluded, and has a more constant temperature. It is also well known and frequently occupied. Also, many of the visitors to Bubbles prefer to go nude.

2

San Francisco Hot Springs

(See map on page 15)

General description: A small group of hot springs bubbling out of the ground into the San Francisco River.

Location: Western New Mexico, near the small towns of Glenwood and Pleasanton.

Primitive/developed: Primitive. Someone has lined the pools with rocks.

Best time of year: Spring, summer, and fall. During winter roads can be too wet, and the river water can make the pools too cold to be enjoyable.

Restrictions: The hot springs themselves are on national forest property. However, private property is adjacent. Several areas are off-limits to vehicle access and camping. Be sure to obey all signs.

Access: The hot springs are accessible via a short drive down a dirt road off U.S. Highway 180, followed by a short walk. The road is usually easily passable by most vehicles, but it can become impassable when wet.

Water temperature: The source averages about 110 degrees F, cooling as it mixes with the river water.

Nearby attractions: San Francisco River, Mogollon.

Services: Gas, food, and lodging can be found in Glenwood, about 4.5 miles to the northeast.

Camping: Camping is not permitted at the hot springs themselves. Undeveloped camping is permitted 0.25 mile farther south along the river. There are also several USDA Forest Service campgrounds north along US 180.

Map: USGS Dillon Mountain, New Mexico quadrangle (1:24,000 scale).

Finding the spring: From the small town of Pleasanton, travel south on US 180 for about 2 miles. Keep an eye out with a pair of binoculars for a small Forest Service sign. A narrow gravel road is on your right immediately past this sign. If driving north on US 180, look for a similar sign on the left side of the road after crossing a bridge. This was the old access route to the springs. Now, however, property owners have restricted access, and you must drive another 2 miles south on US 180 (south of the bridge over Dugway Wash) to an unsigned dirt road on the west side of the highway. You'll have to open a cattle gate; be sure to close it after driving through. Drive about 1 mile along this road, heading for a corral (staying right at a Y intersection). Park near the corral and look for a small trail to the west. Take the trail for about 1.25 miles down to the river. The last part of the trail is rather steep, so be careful. The trail will take you directly to Bubbles Hot Springs. San Francisco Hot Springs is located about half a mile farther upstream, on the east side of the river adjacent to private land. You will have to cross the river at least two times to reach San Francisco Hot Springs, so be prepared. Do not attemp the crossing during high water levels.

The hot springs: The hot springs bubble up out of the ground adjacent to the San Francisco River at about 110 degrees F. Several primitive, ephemeral rock-lined tubs have been constructed around the hot springs to form small baths. The hot water is mixed with the river water in these makeshift pools. During high water, the pools are generally washed out. A few years ago, the hot springs were accessible from the dirt road described above and a short walk. Recent changes in property ownership, however, have resulted in the closure of this access. The USDA Forest Service opened another route, described above, to alleviate this problem. Whatever you do, obey all "No Trespassing" signs and do not cross private property to reach the springs. Located a short distance off the highway, San Francisco Hot Springs is rather well known and sees a high volume of visitors. The rock-lined pools are in the open, and not exactly secluded. Nevertheless, many visitors prefer to go nude. The Forest Service, however, prohibits nude bathing in this location and has been known to issue citations, but enforcement of the no nude bathing regulation is rather lax. Although you may have to share the hot springs with others, the San Francisco River area is beautiful and enjoyable. Other hot springs, including Bubbles, are close by and easy to get to.

Mogollon: Definitely a ghost town worth seeing, Mogollon is a long drive on a dirt road replete with hairpin turns. Founded in the 1890s, Mogollon

San Francisco Hot Springs.

quickly rose to prominence due to its silver and gold ore, both of which were mined in abundance. The road to the town was actually constructed in 1897 by convict labor as were many roads during that time. In places, the road had to be hacked out of the hillside. Teams of 20 mules brought the ore from the mines in Mogollon to be processed elsewhere. The miners not only had to deal with a difficult access route to and from the mines, they were also frequently raided by Apache war parties and many were killed. By 1914, the town supported a payroll of nearly $1 million. But by 1926, like many other mining towns, Magollon declined. World War II brought about the end of mining at Mogollon, and the town all but dried up. Today a few hardy souls remain; please respect their historic area.

From Glenwood, drive 5 miles north on US 180 to a small sign for the road to Mogollon. Turn right (east) and follow the dirt road (New Mexico Highway 159) for about 10 miles to the ghost town. A variety of ruins, buildings, and structures awaits you.

3
Frisco Box Hot Springs

General description: A small concrete pool of warm water alongside the upper San Francisco River in the Gila National Forest's San Francisco Mountains. A moderately strenuous hike is required to reach the springs.
Location: Western New Mexico, east of the small town of Luna.
Primitive/developed: Primitive. The small concrete pool does not detract from the beautiful and natural setting of the hot springs.
Best time of year: Summer and early fall. Located at 6,500 feet, the access road will be closed during most of winter, and the river can be too high during spring runoff.
Restrictions: The hot springs themselves are on national forest property. However, private property is adjacent. Be sure to remain on national forest property by following the route to the springs described here.
Access: The hot springs are accessible via a 12-mile drive down a dirt road followed by a moderately strenuous hike of 3 miles (with an elevation change of 1,600 feet.). The road is usually passable to most vehicles with decent clearance, but it can become impassable when wet.
Water temperature: The source is about 98 degrees F, and becomes cooler in the concrete tub.
Nearby attractions: The Box, Bubbles Hot Springs, San Francisco Hot Springs.
Services: Gas, food, and lodging can be found in Alpine, Arizona, about 30 miles to the west. Luna has a general store.
Camping: Camping is permitted in the forest surrounding the hot springs; just be sure you're on national forest property. There are several USDA Forest Service campgrounds in the Gila National Forest; contact the Luna Ranger District for more information and locations.
Map: USGS Dillon Mountain, New Mexico quadrangle (1:24,000 scale).

Finding the spring: From Luna, New Mexico, take U.S. Highway 180 south for about 6.5 miles to Forest Road 35, on your left. Take FR 35 (a graded dirt road) for 12 miles to its end at a metal gate. Park at the gate, then backtrack slightly to the saddle of the mountain and look for a small wooden trail sign to the north (you may have to hunt around to find it). The trailhead for the Frisco Divide Trail 124 is located at the top of the ridge at what's known as the H Bar V Saddle.

You now have a 3.5-mile hike ahead of you, with an elevation change of 1,600 feet. Follow Divide Trail 124 as it runs along the ridge for less than 1 mile, then descends rapidly to reach the canyon of the San Francisco River.

Frisco Box Hot Springs

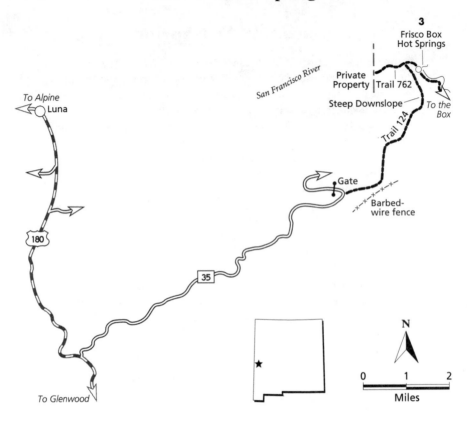

The way down is steep, so use care. Although there is only one trail, it can be hard to follow at times. The Forest Service has attempted to improve it and in some places has marked it with flagging or stone markers. After 3 miles you reach the canyon bottom and Frisco Box Trail 762. Turn right (east) and follow this trail for about half a mile. The trail crosses the San Francisco River at least twice, but keep looking for a small concrete pool on the river's south bank. It is not always easy to find, so keep your eyes open.

The hot springs: Frisco Box Hot Springs is actually more of a warm spring because the 98 degree F water cools off considerably in the small concrete tub. The tub captures one of several small hot-spring seeps along the banks of the San Francisco River.

The challenging hike required to reach the springs makes it that much more enjoyable. Unfortunately, you have all the uphill part of the hike on your way out. Be sure to leave plenty of water, food, strength, and sunlight for the return trip. Also, plan that your return will take twice as long.

Set in the high pine forest of the San Francisco Mountains, Frisco Box Hot Springs is a great spring to visit if you like wilderness solitude. A previous access route required a much shorter hike and resulted in many more visitors. Following problems between visitors to the springs and local landowners, the route was closed. The Forest Service then opened the route described here, which follows infrequently used pack trails.

If you have time, be sure to visit the Box, which is where the San Francisco River is constricted into an extremely narrow canyon, just 1 mile farther from the hot springs. The best way to visit both the Box and the hot springs is to backpack and camp somewhere along the river. Trying to do both in a day trip can be too much. For further information and access issues, contact the Gila National Forest's Luna Ranger Station at 505-533-6232.

4

Faywood Hot Springs

General description: A historic hot-spring resort, recently renovated to provide an excellent bathing experience.

Location: Southwestern New Mexico, northwest of the town of Deming.

Primitive/developed: Developed, but rustic. This is a no-frills resort; the only development consists of the pools.

Best time of year: Fall, winter, and spring. Summer is too hot.

Restrictions: This is private property, and the pools are open only to registered guests. The gate is locked between 10 P.M. and 8 A.M.

Access: The resort is located immediately off U.S. Highway 180 and is accessible by virtually any vehicle.

Water temperature: The source is about 129 degrees F. The pools vary in temperature, from about 95 to 110 degrees F. The private tubs temperatures can be regulated by the user.

Nearby attractions: Gila Wilderness, Silver City.

Services: Gas, food, and lodging can be found in Deming, about 26 miles to the southeast.

Faywood Hot Springs

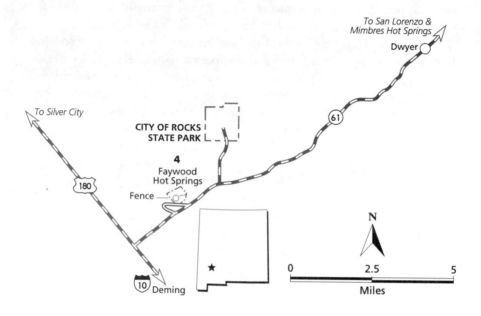

Camping: Camping options at Faywood include tent and RV sites, a tepee, and several travel trailers.
Map: USGS Hatch, New Mexico quadrangle (1:100,000 scale).

Finding the spring: From Deming, head northwest on US 180 for about 24 miles to a sign for the City of Rocks State Park. Turn right (east) on New Mexico Highway 61 and drive about 2 miles to the signs for Faywood on the left. Turn left onto the small dirt road and follow it to the resort office.

The hot springs: Faywood is a enjoyable bathing experience thanks to the current owners, who have done an excellent job of renovating the pools. The natural hot water flows out of the top of a hill at about 129 degrees F. From there the water is diverted into several pool areas, where it cools off. With both clothing and clothing-optional bathing areas, as well as private tubs, the resort offers a wide variety of choices. Each area has several bathing pools of varying sizes and temperatures. The grounds around the pools are well vegetated, with paths throughout. As a bonus, there are many friendly cats prowling the grounds.

Day use of the pools is available for $7.50 per hour ($3.75 child) or $10 per day ($5 child). Private pools are $20 per hour, and private tubs are $10 per hour. Group discounts and frequent-user rates are also available. Faywood Hot Springs can be reached at 505-536-9663, or e-mail: faywood@faywood.com.

The hot springs at Faywood have been well known for countless centuries. The springs were well used by Native Americans, as the mortar holes for grinding seeds and other foodstuffs attest. Evidence suggests the ancient Mimbres culture used the springs, as well as the more recent Apache. The springs are mentioned in many early Euro-American accounts of travel through the area. This is not surprising, as the springs are located along a once major travel corridor between what is now New Mexico and Arizona. The springs were first commercially used in 1876 when Colonel Richard Hudson constructed the Hudson Hotel there. Many people journeyed there for enjoyment as well as to cure a variety of ailments. Unfortunately, the hotel burned down in 1892, but in 1894, another hotel was built, this one much larger. Andrew Graham's Casa de Consuelo (House of Comfort) had 60 rooms. Its luxuriance attests to the popularity of hot springs in the late nineteenth century, and to the belief in mineral water's curative abilities.

Near the turn of the century, three men, T. C. McDermott, J. C. Fay, and W. Lockwood, purchased the resort and named it Faywood. Throughout the next few decades, Faywood enjoyed a popularity not found at most other hot-spring resorts. Many people from Silver City and Deming made regular trips to visit the springs. Like others, however, Faywood also declined in popularity, and by 1951 the buildings were destroyed. The property passed through many hands until Kennecott Copper acquired it in 1966. The current owners purchased the springs from the Phelps Dodge Company in 1993.

5

Mimbres Hot Springs

General description: A collection of high-temperature hot springs serving a private community in a beautiful canyon setting.

Location: Southwestern New Mexico, about 45 miles north of Deming and 35 miles east of Silver City.

Primitive/developed: Developed. The hot water at this location has been harnessed for many years, although it is currently closed to the public.

Best time of year: Fall, spring, and summer. Winter snows can make the road too muddy.

Mimbres Hot Springs

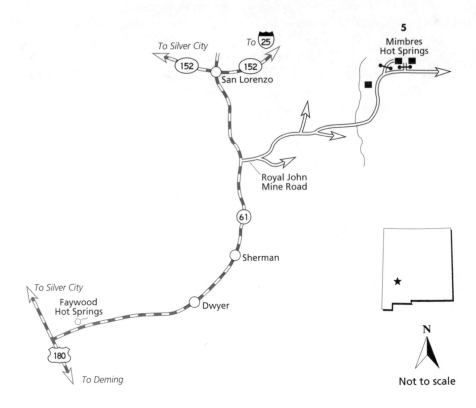

Restrictions: This is private property; be sure to obey all posted signs. All visitors must have a resident sponsor to escort them onto the property.

Access: Located on a well-maintained dirt road, the springs can be reached by most vehicles with normal clearance.

Water temperature: The source is about 136 degrees F, but it's cooler in the various tubs.

Nearby attractions: Gila Wilderness, Faywood Hot Springs.

Services: The nearest services are in Deming and Silver City.

Camping: Camping is not permitted at Mimbres. There is camping at Faywood Hot Springs, about 20 miles away, and plenty of undeveloped camping opportunities in the nearby Gila National Forest.

Map: USGS Hatch, New Mexico quadrangle (1:100,000 scale).

Finding the spring: From Deming, travel northwest on U.S. Highway 180 for about 24 miles to New Mexico Highway 61, where you turn right (east). Travel on NM 61 for about 20 miles (passing Faywood Hot Springs) to Royal

John Mine Road, where you turn right (east). Follow the main road for 1 mile, then bear right at Hot Springs Canyon Road. Continue another 0.2 mile, then bear left. Continue another mile (crossing a one-lane bridge) until you reach Mimbres Hot Springs on your left.

The hot springs: Set in a beautiful canyon in the foothills of the Gila Mountains of southern New Mexico, Mimbres Hot Springs is a fantastic collection of springs. All of the springs have been harnessed and feed several tubs. Although it has passed through various hands during its lifetime, Mimbres Hot Springs is currently closed to the general public. The only way to visit the springs is to be accompanied by a resident. The springs may, however, open to the public eventually. In the meantime, please obey all posted signs, and do not trespass. Also, do not try to reach the springs if the road is muddy; you may get stuck.

6

Radium Springs

General description: A historic hot-spring resort alongside the Rio Grande. Although it has been closed for years, it is hoped that someday the resort will be reopened into a bed and breakfast.

Location: Southern New Mexico, outside the small town of Radium Springs, along Interstate 25 northwest of Las Cruces.

Primitive/developed: Developed. The hot water at this location has been harnessed for many years, although it is currently closed to the public.

Best time of year: Fall, winter, and spring. Summer is too hot, with daytime temperatures often topping 120 degrees F.

Restrictions: This is private property; be sure to obey all posted signs.

Access: The resort can be reached via a paved road.

Water temperature: The source is about 127 degrees F.

Nearby attractions: Elephant Butte Reservoir.

Services: Gas and food can be found in Fort Selden, immediately off the interstate. More complete services can be found in Las Cruces, about 25 miles to the southeast.

Camping: Camping is not permitted at Radium Springs or in the immediate vicinity. A state campground is located at nearby Fort Selden.

Map: New Mexico State Highway Map.

Radium Springs

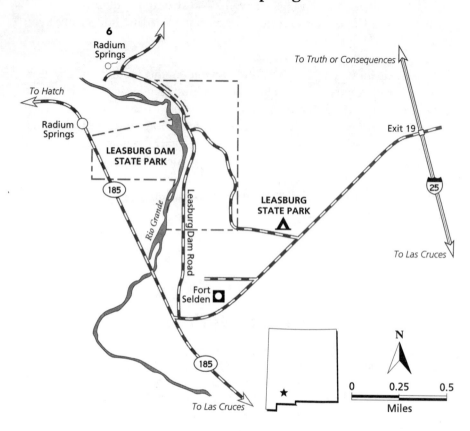

Finding the spring: From Las Cruces, travel northwest on I-25 for about 15 miles to exit 19 at Leasburg Dam Road. Exit here and head west past Fort Selden State Park. Turn right on Leasburg Dam Road, the last intersection before you come to New Mexico Highway 185. Follow this narrow paved road for less than 2 miles and cross a bridge to where the road splits. To the right is a dirt road (which goes under a railroad bridge); straight ahead is Radium Springs Resort.

The hot springs: Radium has a rich history. Located along an important historic travel corridor, the hot springs at Radium have likely been known for centuries. Originally, the springs were called Selden Springs. With the arrival of the railroad in the late nineteenth century, however, the springs received a great deal more attention. The Santa Fe Railroad constructed a Harvey House here, but the most well-known resort was built by Harry Bailey in 1931. Bailey, who was a friend of New Mexico luminaries Billy the Kid and Pat Garrett, constructed a bathhouse and hotel on the site, and it became known as Bailey's Baths. As the popularity of hot springs declined in the 1940s and 1950s, the property fell into disuse. The next occupant was the state of New Mexico, in the form of a women's prison, which was short-lived. Another resort was attempted in the early 1980s by the Daly family. A swimming pool, several individual hot tubs, and steam baths, and even a Hungarian restaurant were in the resort.

Unfortunately, the resort is closed today. There is hope that it will reopen someday, but no one seems to be sure. For up-to-date information, write Radium Springs Resort, P.O. Box 35, Radium Springs, NM 88054.

Fort Selden: Fort Selden was established in 1865 to protect travel along the important Camino Real de Tierra Adentro, a route along the Rio Grande that was vital to Spanish, Mexican, and American trade and communications. The fort was abandoned in 1878, only to be reconstructed and reoccupied in 1881. In 1891 it was permanently abandoned, and the property went into private hands. In 1963 it was donated to the state of New Mexico. In 1974, the site was declared a state monument, and restoration work on the adobe buildings began. Recently, the fort has been the location of several experimental adobe restoration practices. Several agencies have been involved with the preservation efforts, including the Getty Conservation Institute.

GILA WILDERNESS AREA

Designated as the nation's first wilderness area in 1924, the Gila Wilderness has not changed much since. If you enjoy unspoiled wilderness far from civilization and relatively free of people, this is the place for you. The Gila Wilderness Area is surrounded by the Gila National Forest, which contains everything from low desert scrub to high pine forests. This is the headwaters of the mighty Gila River, which flows across the entire state of Arizona, eventually reaching the Colorado River at the California–Arizona state line. The Gila Wilderness is a haven for hot springs. The Gila Mountains are volcanic in origin, having in geologic time only recently been formed. The volcanic activity in the area explains the plethora of hot springs in a relatively small geographic area. The hot springs themselves occur along a regular north-south trend, formed by hot water at depth and forced to the surface along a few fault lines.

Ample recreational opportunities are available here, including hiking, backpacking, fishing, and horseback riding. The area is also rich in wildlife, particularly birds. The archaeological wealth of the area is capped by the Gila Cliff Dwellings, located at the northern end of New Mexico Highway 15, near the community of Gila Hot Springs. You can reach Gila Hot Springs by traveling north from Silver City for 39 miles on NM 15. It's a slow drive (at least two hours) because of its countless hairpin turns. The town offers only the most basic amenities, including a general store, camping, and limited lodging. Pack trips can be organized here, however, and you can get information on the area in general.

Doc Campbell came to the area in 1935, ranching cattle at first, and eventually advertising the hot springs of the area. In 1940 he acquired much of the property encompassing the Gila Hot Springs area. The hot-spring water supplied his ranch, as well as a natural spa, which he opened to the public. A paved automobile road to the Gila Hot Springs area was built in 1966; prior to that one had to follow treacherous trails and, for a while, a difficult dirt road. The difficulty in reaching the area maintained its isolation for years. Another hot-spring lodge—the Lyons Lodge—also existed along the banks of the Gila River. Built by wealthy cattle rancher Thomas Lyons, it was located next to a hot spring on the East Fork of the Gila River. The lodge was elaborate and hosted many famous people who sought the solitude of the wilderness. Building materials as well as furnishings for this grand lodge were brought to the area by mule train, taking several days from Silver City. The Lyons Lodge is closed, and is not accessible to the public.

You can still visit Doc Campbell's Trading Post, where you can stock up with supplies. Many of the area's hot springs can still be enjoyed, including those at the Gila River Campground, as well as the RV park across the road. To reach the Gila Hot Springs Vacation Center, call 505-536-9551.

For the latest access information on backcountry hot springs, as well as trail conditions and weather, call the Gila Wilderness Ranger District at 505-536-2250.

7

Melanie Hot Springs

General description: A fantastic set of natural hot springs alongside a remote portion of the upper Gila River. Bathing opportunities include three small rock pools and a small, warm waterfall.

Location: Southwestern New Mexico, south of the small community of Gila Hot Springs.

Primitive/developed: Primitive. The only development has been the creation of small soaking pools

Best time of year: Summer and early fall. Due to its high elevation, the road to the springs can be treacherous during winter. The Gila River can be too high in the spring to be safe for the many crossings required.

Restrictions: The hot springs are located in the Gila National Forest in a designated wilderness area. Motorized vehicles, which would be impossible to operate in this rugged area anyway, are prohibited.

Access: Melanie Hot Springs can be reached only by foot or horseback, down a 1.5-mile trail that crosses the Gila River eight times.

Water temperature: The source is about 111 degrees F. The water cools off to about 98 degrees in the small pools and warm waterfall.

Nearby attractions: Gila Hot Springs, Middlefork (Lightfeather) Hot Springs, Gila Cliff Dwellings.

Services: Gas and food can be found in Gila Hot Springs, about 3 miles to the north. This is a very small town, however, and you must go to Silver City for more complete services (about 39 miles south).

Camping: There is an RV campground in Gila Hot Springs, along with an undeveloped private campground. An undeveloped USDA Forest Service campground is located at the trailhead to the hot springs, and two Forest Service campgrounds are located near the Gila Cliff Dwellings.

Map: USGS Gila Hot Springs, New Mexico quadrangle (1:24,000 scale).

Finding the spring: From Silver City, travel north on New Mexico Highway 15 to Pinos Altos. Stay on NM 15 (through Pinos Altos) for about 37.5 miles into the Gila Wilderness. Immediately prior to crossing the Gila River, there is a dirt road leading to a campground on your right; turn off the highway here. As you drive down the dirt road, stay to the left for the trailhead parking lot (the campground is to the right). Park here and get ready to hike. Follow a faint trail that leads under the highway bridge and crosses the river immediately. The trail crosses the river eight times before reaching the hot springs, and it can be hard to spot sometimes. You may end up crossing the river more or less than eight times if you wander off the trail. As long as the river is not too high, it doesn't matter too much. Keep an eye on the left (west) bank of the river for extra foliage growing where the hot springs emanate. You have gone too far if you get to a large bend in the river forming a horseshoe shape. The hot springs are upstream about 100 yards from this bend.

The hot springs: Melanie Hot Springs consists of two small seeps in a steep hillside overlooking the Gila River. The sources are obscured by vegetation, but they flow into three small pools. The first pool is actually a little grotto, with only about 2-foot-deep warm water. The other two pools are at the base of the cliff and were created by volunteers with rocks and sand. The hot

Gila River below Melanie Hot Springs.

Melanie Hot Springs

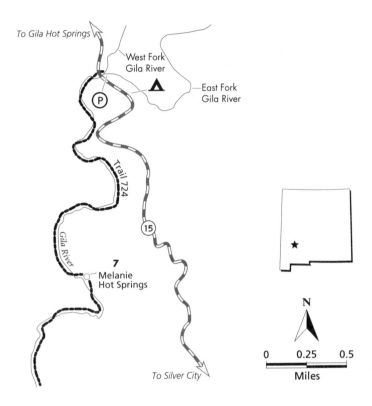

springs also form a small, warm waterfall between the grotto and the pools. Sometimes, the water flows into the Gila River, where people often build small pools to mix the warm water with the cold river water. Don't count on this, however, as a way to find the hot springs. Often, there is insufficient water to flow all the way to the river.

8

Gila Hot Springs

General description: A collection of high-temperature hot springs alongside the West Fork of the Gila River.

Location: Southwestern New Mexico, in the small community of Gila Hot Springs.

Primitive/developed: Primitive. The hot-spring sources are closed to the public, but the hot water has been piped across the river to serve several pools in a campground.

Best time of year: Late spring, summer, and early fall. Because Gila Hot Springs is located at high elevation, road conditions can be treacherous and occasionally impassable in winter.

Restrictions: The springs are located on private property. The pools in the campground can be used by campers or day users for $2. Be sure to obey all campground regulations.

Access: The hot springs are located a short distance off New Mexico Highway 15 on a dirt road. Most cars should have no trouble reaching the springs. The road may be impassable when wet, however.

Water temperature: The source is about 150 degrees F. The water cools off to about 110 degrees F in the larger pool, and somewhat higher and lower in the other pools.

Nearby attractions: Melanie Hot Springs, Middlefork Lightfeather Hot Springs, Gila Cliff Dwellings.

Services: Gas and food can be found in the town of Gila Hot Springs, less than 1 mile to the north. This is a very small town, however, and you must go to Silver City for more complete services (about 39 miles south).

Camping: The small campground at Gila Hot Springs is privately owned. It has pit toilets and water. There is an RV campground across NM 15 in the town of Gila Hot Springs. Several USDA Forest Service campgrounds are located near the Gila Cliff Dwellings.

Map: USGS Gila Hot Springs, New Mexico quadrangle (1:24,000 scale).

Finding the spring: From Silver City, travel north on NM 15 to Pinos Altos. Stay on NM 15 (through Pinos Altos) for about 38 miles into the Gila Wilderness. Immediately before you reach the small community of Gila Hot Springs, keep an eye out for a sign for the Gila River Campground. Turn right at the sign onto Access Road. Take the dirt road downhill for about a quarter of a mile, then turn left to the river and the campground. Follow the signs.

Gila Hot Springs
Wildwood Hot Springs
Gila Hot Springs RV Park

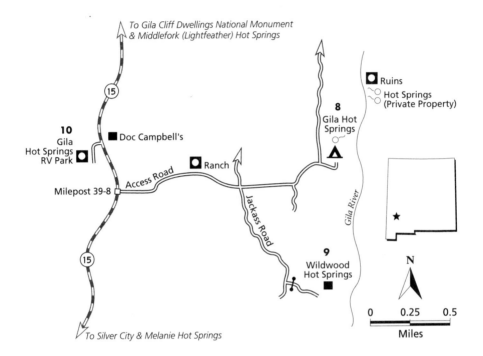

The hot springs: The actual springs at Gila Hot Springs are located on the other side of the river from the campground. They are, however, on private property that is closed to public access. At one time, the hot springs provided hot water to the town of Gila Hot Springs, and could be accessed by the public. Today, your only option is the campground. The Gila River Campground uses the hot water from these springs by piping it across the river, then underground, and finally to the surface and into several pools of varying temperatures. The pools closest to the campsites are almost scalding, whereas the others are deeper and a little cooler (around 110 degrees F). You can see the Gila Hot Springs themselves from the campground, if you look upstream. Several ruins and foundations can be seen, along with unusual colored rock and travertine. Unimproved camping is available for $3 per night; day use is $2. Pit toilets and water are available. The setting is fantastic, located on the banks of the rushing Gila River.

9

Wildwood Hot Springs

(See map on page 33)

General description: A once open, but now closed private hot-spring resort alongside the Gila River.

Location: Southwestern New Mexico, southeast of the small community of Gila Hot Springs.

Primitive/developed: At one time Wildwood was a developed resort, but now it has fallen into disuse and deteriorated substantially.

Best time of year: Late spring, summer, and early fall. Because Wildwood is located high in the mountains, road conditions can be treacherous and occasionally impassable in winter.

Restrictions: The springs are located on private property and are currently closed to public use. Be sure to obey all "No Trespassing" signs.

Access: The hot springs are located a short distance off New Mexico Highway 15 on a dirt road.

Water temperature: The source is about 110 degrees F.

Nearby attractions: Melanie Hot Springs, Middlefork (Lightfeather) Hot Springs, Gila Hot Springs, Gila Cliff Dwellings.

Services: Gas and food can be found in Gila Hot Springs, about 2 miles to the northwest. This is a very small town, however, and you must go to Silver City for more complete services (about 39 miles south).

Camping: The campground at Gila Hot Springs has pit toilets and water. There is an RV campground across NM 15 in the town of Gila Hot Springs. Several USDA Forest Service campgrounds are located near the Gila Cliff Dwellings.

Map: USGS Gila Hot Springs, New Mexico quadrangle (1:24,000 scale).

Finding the spring: From Silver City, travel north on NM 15 to Pinos Altos. Stay on NM 15 (through Pinos Altos) for about 38 miles into the Gila Wilderness. Immediately prior to reaching the small community of Gila Hot Springs, keep an eye out for a sign for the Gila Hot Springs Campground. Turn right at the sign onto Access Road. Take the dirt road downhill past a ranch and turn right onto another dirt road, Jackass Road. Follow this road to its end, about half a mile.

The hot springs: At one time Wildwood Hot Springs was just one of several resorts in the Gila Hot Springs area. Unfortunately, many of these hot-spring resorts have gone out of business. Although you can't currently visit

Wildwood Hot Springs, it is included here in the hope that it will open again soon. Keep an eye out for signs indicating its reopening, should it ever happen.

10

Gila Hot Springs RV Park

(See map on page 33)

General description: A semideveloped RV park complete with hot-spring baths.

Location: Southwestern New Mexico, in the small community of Gila Hot Springs.

Primitive/developed: Developed. The hot springs are piped into a small bath facility. RV hookups and campsites are available.

Best time of year: Late spring, summer, and early fall. Because Gila Hot Springs is located high in the mountains, road conditions can be treacherous and occasionally impassable in winter.

Restrictions: The springs are located on private property. Be sure to pay all use fees and obey all posted rules.

Gila Hot Springs campground.

Access: The hot springs are located immediately off New Mexico Highway 15.

Water temperature: The source is about120 degrees F. The water cools off in the baths, however.

Nearby attractions: Melanie Hot Springs, Gila Hot Springs, Middlefork Lightfeather Hot Springs, Gila Cliff Dwellings.

Services: Gas and food can be found in Gila Hot Springs. This is a very small town, however, and you must go to Silver City for more complete services (about 39 miles south). The RV park does offer a few furnished apartments; call 505-536-9340 for reservations and rates.

Camping: Tent camping is $9 and RV hookups are $15 at the RV park. Several USDA Forest Service campgrounds are located near the Gila Cliff Dwellings.

Map: USGS Gila Hot Springs, New Mexico quadrangle (1:24,000 scale).

Finding the spring: From Silver City, travel north on NM 15 to Pinos Altos. Stay on NM 15 (through Pinos Altos) for about 39 miles to the community of Gila Hot Springs. Keep an eye out for a sign for the RV park on your left, immediately off the highway.

The hot springs: For those with RVs, or those desiring a little more in the way of civilized comforts, the Gila Hot Springs RV Park offers the best alternative. Tent camping is $9, RV hookups are $15, and there are furnished apartments. The park also offers a nice mineral water bath, as well as showers. Be sure to phone 505-536-9340 for current rates and reservations.

11

Middlefork (Lightfeather) Hot Springs

General description: A wonderful collection of hot springs alongside the Middlefork of the Gila River. The hot springs are located in a wilderness area, requiring a short hike to reach them.

Location: Southwestern New Mexico, north of the small community of Gila Hot Springs.

Primitive/developed: Primitive. The only development consists of rock-lined bathing pools, which are occasionally washed out by flooding.

Best time of year: Late spring, summer, and early fall. Because the hot springs are located high in the mountains, road conditions can be treacherous and occasionally impassable in winter. Also, the Middlefork of the

Middlefork (Lightfeather) Hot Springs

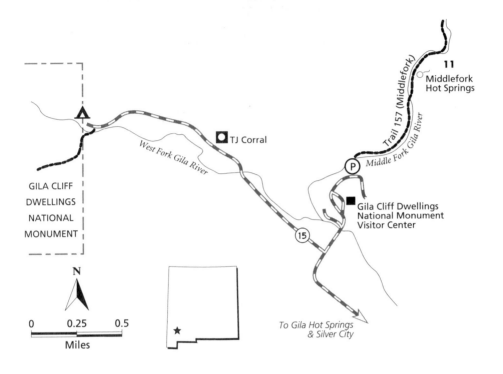

Gila River may be treacherous during high runoff. Do' not attempt to reach the hot springs during this time of year.

Restrictions: The springs are located within the Gila Wilderness, which means that no motorized vehicles are allowed. Otherwise, there are no restrictions.

Access: A hike of about half a mile, which includes at least two river crossings, is required to reach the hot springs.

Water temperature: The source is about149 degrees F. The water cools off as it mixes with the river water in the rock-lined pools. The temperature in the pools will vary depending upon the mixture of hot and cold water.

Nearby attractions: Melanie Hot Springs, Gila Hot Springs, Gila Cliff Dwellings.

Services: Gas and food can be found in Gila Hot Springs. This is a very small town, however, and you must go to Silver City for more complete services (about 39 miles south).

Camping: The Gila Hot Springs Campground is a short drive south along New Mexico Highway 15 and offers riverside camping complete with natural hot-water baths. The Gila Hot Springs RV Park offers tent camping for $9 and RV hookups for $15. Several USDA Forest Service campgrounds are located near the Gila Cliff Dwellings.

Map: USGS Gila Hot Springs, New Mexico quadrangle (1:24,000 scale).

Finding the spring: From Silver City, travel north on NM 15 to Pinos Altos. Stay on NM 15 (through Pinos Altos) for about 39 miles to the community of Gila Hot Springs. Continue through town, following signs for the Gila Cliff Dwellings National Monument. Stay on NM 15 for 2 more miles, then turn right to the visitor center (going straight takes you to the cliff dwellings themselves). Stop in at the visitor center for up-to-date information on river levels and access issues. Continue through the visitor center parking lot and look for a dirt parking lot for the trailhead to Forest Service Trail 157, the Middlefork Trail. Park here and pick up the trail at the end of the parking lot.

The trail leads you down to the Middlefork of the Gila River, which you soon cross. Continue another 0.25 mile on the other side. The trail crosses the river again. From the second crossing, continue less than 0.25 mile upstream, keeping an eye out on the right (east) bank of the river. Slightly upstream of a small rock overhang you will see the small hot-spring source flowing into the river. There may be rock-lined pools in the river, depending upon the time of year.

The hot springs: Middlefork (sometimes referred to as Lightfeather) is a wonderful hot springs to visit, requiring a short but wet hike. There is no way to avoid crossing the river twice. The hot springs themselves are very hot (about 149 degrees F) and will scald you if you sample them near the source. The only way to enjoy the hot water is in one of the rather ephemeral rock-lined pools along the river. The hot-spring water mixes with the cold river water, making for a comfortable bath. During high river levels, however, the pools will be washed out and leave you with no bathing options. Try to visit the springs during the late summer or early fall. Despite its rather isolated location, Middlefork Hot Springs is frequently visited because it's well known and located on a well-traveled trail into the Gila Wilderness backcountry. Don't be surprised by the presence of other hikers or riders on horseback.

Legend states that the famed Apache leader Geronimo was born at these hot springs. Although more modern scholarship places his birthplace closer to Clifton, Arizona, Apache presence in this area is unmistakable. Spanish journals, as well as more recent Anglo accounts, also indicate the presence of the Apache in these mountains. The hot springs in this area were used by the

Apache, and at one time a small structure was built over Middlefork Hot Springs and used by the Apache for bathing. Thankfully, the area has changed little since that time.

12

Jordan Hot Springs

General description: An extremely remote series of hot springs in the Gila Wilderness of the Mogollon Mountains, requiring a difficult hike to reach.

Location: Southwestern New Mexico, in the remote Gila Wilderness, near the community of Gila Hot Springs.

Primitive/developed: Primitive. The only development has been the creation of bathing pools.

Best time of year: Late spring, summer, and early fall. The hot springs are located high in the Mogollon Mountains, along the Middlefork of the Gila River, and are accessible only when the Gila River is low. The best times to do this hike are in late summer and early fall.

Restrictions: The springs are located within the Gila Wilderness. Motorized vehicles, which would be impossible to operate in this rugged area anyway, are prohibited.

Access: A 6-mile (one way) hike is required to reach the hot springs. The last 2 miles require walking in and out of the Middlefork of the Gila River.

Water temperature: The source is about 94 degrees F, making Jordan more of a warm springs. This temperature makes for an excellent bathing experience.

Nearby attractions: The Meadows Warm Springs, Gila Hot Springs, Middlefork (Lightfeather) Hot Springs, Gila Cliff Dwellings.

Services: Gas and food can be found in Gila Hot Springs. This is a very small town, however, and you must go to Silver City for more complete services (about 39 miles south).

Camping: Undeveloped camping is permitted within the wilderness area. Several developed campgrounds are located in the Gila Hot Springs area. There are also several USDA Forest Service campgrounds near the Gila Cliff Dwellings.

Maps: USGS Gila Hot Springs and Woodland Park, New Mexico quadrangles (1:24,000 scale).

Finding the spring: From Silver City, travel north on New Mexico Highway 15 to Pinos Altos. Stay on NM 15 (through Pinos Altos) for about 39 miles to

Jordan Hot Springs
The Meadows Warm Springs

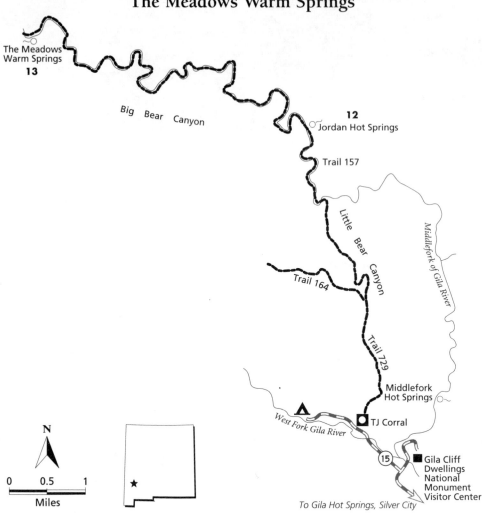

The Meadows
Warm Springs
13

Big Bear Canyon

12
Jordan Hot Springs

Trail 157

Little Bear Canyon

Middlefork of Gila River

Trail 164

Trail 729

Middlefork
Hot Springs

West Fork Gila River

TJ Corral

N

0   0.5   1
Miles

★

15   Gila Cliff
Dwellings
National
Monument
Visitor Center

To Gila Hot Springs, Silver City

the small community of Gila Hot Springs. Continue through town, following signs for the Gila Cliff Dwellings National Monument. Stay on NM 15 for 2 more miles, then turn right to the visitor center (going straight takes you to the cliff dwellings themselves). Stop in at the visitor center for up-to-date information on river levels and access issues. Go back toward the Gila Cliff Dwellings; about 1 mile from the intersection with the road to the visitor center, you will see a pullout for TJ Corral. Turn right here and park at the trailhead.

Take Bear Canyon Trail 729 north, uphill. You climb almost 1,000 feet on this trail for the first 2 miles. The intersection with Trail 164 on your left is at the summit of this climb; continue straight on Trail 729. The trail then descends into the canyon of the Middlefork of the Gila River. In the canyon, the trail intersects with Middlefork Trail 157, which you take to the left (you are now 4 miles from TJ Corral). The Middlefork Trail follows the river, and several crossings will be required. Hike for about 2 miles upstream to reach Jordan Hot Springs. You will cross the river about 15 times before reaching Jordan. The springs are sometimes difficult to find. Look for small pools of warm water adjacent to the river; the springs and the hot bath are about 100 feet above the river. Start looking for the springs when the river makes a broad meander after the fifteenth crossing. You should also be able to notice the dark green vegetation growing near the springs.

The other route to the springs is longer and more difficult. An 8-mile hike from the visitor center, up the Middlefork of the Gila River (past Middlefork Hot Springs) can take you to Jordan, too. Because of the many stream crossings on this journey, however, it is much slower than the one described above. This is definitely a hike you can't do in one day. If you take this route, just keep an eye out for Bear Canyon coming in from the left at 6 miles, and look for the hot springs another 2 miles up the canyon. It's more difficult than it sounds, however, as crossing the river will slow you down considerably.

The hot springs: Jordan Hot Springs is one of the better backcountry hot springs in the West. A series of small, warm springs feed into a rock pool that is deep and wide enough to accommodate several bathers. The warm water is ideal after a long hike. The setting is also superb, located along the Middlefork of the Gila River, surrounded by lush vegetation. The distance to the springs is about 6 miles and requires numerous river crossings. This hike is not recommended as a one-day trip. To really enjoy the hot springs, I recommend that you backpack to them and stay a night or two. Despite its remote location, Jordan Hot Springs is rather well known and frequently visited, especially during summer months. Do not expect to have the pool to yourself. Be sure to check in at the Gila Cliff Dwellings National Monument Visitor Center for information on water levels and other access issues. Also, be sure to notify someone of when and where you are going and when you expect to be back. Don't make this trip if water levels are high, or if storms threaten. Flash floods can be deadly in several places along the trail.

There are several other hot and warm springs in the Gila Wilderness area, and you could spend weeks exploring them all. The Meadows Warm Springs are located another 4 miles upstream along the Middlefork of the Gila River, and Middlefork Hot Springs are about 8 miles downstream.

13

The Meadows Warm Springs

(See map on page 40)

General description: An extremely remote collection of warm springs in the Gila Wilderness of the Mogollon Mountains, requiring a difficult hike to reach. No bathing opportunities.

Location: Southwestern New Mexico, in the remote Gila Wilderness, near the small community of Gila Hot Springs.

Primitive/developed: Primitive, no development.

Best time of year: Late spring, summer, and early fall. The hot springs are located high in the Mogollon Mountains, along the Middlefork of the Gila River, and are accessible only when the Gila River is low. The best times to do this hike are in late summer and early fall.

Restrictions: The springs are located within the Gila Wilderness. Motorized vehicles, which would be impossible to operate in this rugged area anyway, are prohibited.

Access: A 10-mile (one way) hike is required to reach the warm springs. The last 6 miles require walking in and out of the Middlefork of the Gila River.

Water temperature: The source is about 91 degrees F.

Nearby attractions: Jordan Hot Springs, Gila Hot Springs, Middlefork (Lightfeather) Hot Springs, Gila Cliff Dwellings.

Services: Gas and food can be found in Gila Hot Springs. This is a very small town, however, and you must go to Silver City for more complete services (about 40 miles south).

Camping: Undeveloped camping is permitted within the wilderness area. Several developed campgrounds are located in the Gila Hot Springs area. There are also several USDA Forest Service campgrounds near the Gila Cliff Dwellings.

Maps: USGS Gila Hot Springs and Woodland Park, New Mexico quadrangles (1:24,000 scale).

Finding the spring: From Silver City, travel north on New Mexico Highway 15 to Pinos Altos. Stay on NM 15 (through Pinos Altos) for about 39 miles to the small community of Gila Hot Springs. Continue through town, following signs for the Gila Cliff Dwellings National Monument. Stay on NM 15 for 2 more miles, then turn right to the visitor center (going straight takes you to the cliff dwellings themselves). Stop in at the visitor center for up-to-date information on river levels and access issues. Go back toward the

Gila Cliff Dwellings; about 1 mile from the intersection with the road to the visitor center, you will see a pullout for TJ Corral. Turn right here and park at the trailhead.

Take the Bear Canyon Trail 729 north, uphill. You climb almost 1,000 feet on this trail for the first 2 miles. The intersection with Trail 164 on your left is at the summit of this climb; continue straight on Trail 729. The trail then descends into the canyon of the Middlefork of the Gila River. In the canyon, the trail intersects with Middlefork Trail 157, which you will take to the left (you are now 4 miles from TJ Corral). The Middlefork Trail follows the river, which you have to cross several times. Hike for about 2 miles upstream to reach Jordan Hot Springs, crossing the river about 15 times.

From Jordan Hot Springs, continue up the Middlefork of the Gila River for another 4 miles. The warm springs are difficult to find, as there are no pools per se. Watch for a large meadow and seeps of warm water along the west bank of the Middlefork. Be sure to bring along a topographic map.

The hot springs: Meadows Warm Springs is located in an even more remote area of the Gila Wilderness and is less frequently visited than Jordan Hot Springs. Part of the reason for this is the lack of bathing opportunities here. The springs are basically seeps of warm water, uncollected in any pools or tubs. The setting is fantastic, however, and is one of the lushest in the wilderness. A large meadow surrounds the warm springs, affording a very pleasing environment. The springs form a marshy area with dark green vegetation in the meadow, but they are difficult to find. Be sure to check in at the visitor center for information on water levels and other access issues. Also, be sure to notify someone of when and where you are going and when you expect to be back. Don't make this trip if water levels are high or if storms threaten. Flash floods can be deadly in several places along the trail.

Gila Cliff Dwellings: Be sure to take some time to visit the 1,000-year-old Gila Cliff Dwellings on your visit to the Gila Wilderness. These two-story structures were occupied by the Mogollon Culture and were quite elaborate when built. Adolph Bandelier, famed southwestern archaeologist, visited the ruins of the dwellings in 1884 and described them in the following way:

"Perfectly sheltered, and therefore quite well preserved, the cave villages are perhaps larger than the open air ruins, compactness compensating for the limitation in space. The buildings occupy four caverns, the second of which towards the east is ten meters high. The western cave communicates with the others only from the outside, while the three eastern ones are separated by huge pillars, behind which are natural passageways from one cave to the other."

To reach the Gila Cliff Dwellings, drive north on New Mexico Highway 15 from the visitor center for another 1.5 miles to the parking lot and trailhead for the cliff dwellings. Park here and pick up the narrow 1-mile trail to the cliff dwellings, which overlook the West Fork of the Gila River.

14

Turkey Creek Hot Springs

General description: An extremely remote hot springs in the Gila Wilderness of the Mogollon Mountains, requiring a difficult drive and hike to reach. Several fantastic bathing opportunities await you after the 4-mile hike, however.

Location: Southwestern New Mexico, in the remote Gila Wilderness, near the town of Cliff.

Primitive/developed: Primitive. There has been no development of the hot springs.

Best time of year: Late spring, summer, and early fall. The hot springs are located high in the Mogollon Mountains, along Turkey Creek, which is a tributary of the Gila River. This area is accessible only during low water levels. The best times to do this hike are in late summer and early fall.

Restrictions: The springs are located within the Gila Wilderness. Motorized vehicles, which would be impossible to operate in this rugged area anyway, are prohibited.

Access: The route to the trailhead for Turkey Creek Hot Springs includes a long and sometimes difficult dirt road, about 9.5 miles from where the pavement ends. From the trailhead, a 4-mile (one way) hike is required to reach the hot springs. The majority of this hike is in and out of Turkey Creek, making it a slow journey.

Water temperature: The source is about 165 degrees F. There are several pools of varying temperatures in which to enjoy the springs, including both hot and warm pools.

Nearby attractions: Mangas Hot Springs, San Francisco Hot Springs, Bubbles Hot Springs.

Services: Gas and food can be found in Gila and Cliff. These are both small towns, however, and have only basic services available. For more complete services (including lodging), drive about 40 miles to Silver City.

Camping: Undeveloped camping is permitted within the wilderness area.

Maps: USGS Canyon Hill and Canteen Canyon, New Mexico quadrangles (1:24,000 scale).

Finding the spring: From Silver City, head northwest on U.S. Highway 180 for about 29 miles to New Mexico Highway 211. Turn right (east) toward the town of Gila. Drive on NM 211 for 4 miles, then continue straight on NM 153 as NM 211 bears left. Continue on NM 153 for 4 miles until the pavement ends. The road is now labeled Forest Road 155. Drive about 9.5 miles along this dirt road, which gets steadily worse. Follow it to its end at the Gila River, and park. From here, you begin your long and challenging hike.

Several trails leave from the parking area and follow the Gila River upstream. Follow the main route (which is often marked by vehicle tracks) as it goes in and out of the Gila River several times. You have about 1 mile of hiking, which includes three crossings of the Gila River to reach the mouth of

Turkey Creek Hot Springs

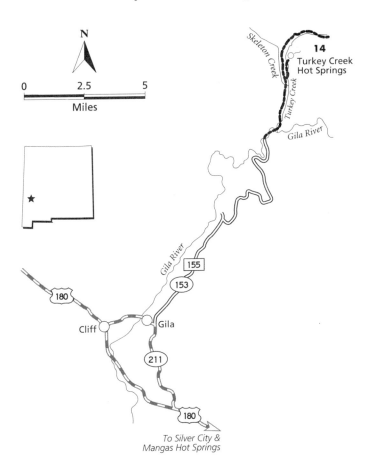

Turkey Creek. The creek will generally be dry where it intersects the Gila River. Just follow the main trail up the creek, passing several old buildings and a windmill in less than 0.25 mile. The trail soon crosses Turkey Creek, which may have water. Follow the trail up Turkey Creek for another 2 miles. The first Y intersection in the trail occurs about 2 miles up the canyon, one fork going over a low cliff and the other staying along the creek. You may take either one, because they rejoin shortly. Soon thereafter, however, Skeleton Canyon trail joins Turkey Creek trail on the left. Be sure to bear right at this unsigned intersection, staying in the Turkey Creek drainage. The Skeleton Canyon Trail heads uphill out of the canyon almost immediately, so you know you have gone the wrong way if you find yourself on this trail.

The last mile to the hot springs is the slowest and most difficult part. Although several trails head upstream, you are pretty much on your own in finding a route. You have to ford the creek and occasionally even wade through large pools. Keep an eye out for faint trails on your right after traveling for about a mile. You may see algae growth as well as greener vegetation, indicating the presence of the springs. You will have to hunt around in this area to find the springs seeping into the creek. There are a few obvious rock-lined pools, but you should be able to feel the water temperature changes brought on by the hot water mixing with the creek water.

The hot springs: Turkey Creek Hot Springs is not easy to reach, and can be difficult to locate. This keeps most casual visitors away. For those looking for a challenging hike and a little bit of hot-spring hunting, Turkey Creek Hot Springs is fantastic. Although the hot springs themselves are very hot at 165 degrees F, they are obscured by Turkey Creek. Rock-lined pools are occasionally built in the creekbed to trap the hot water, but they're frequently washed out. There is one large swimming hole that has substantial amounts of hot-spring seepage, making the temperature quite warm. Soaking pools will vary depending upon what volunteers have built at Turkey Creek, but you can usually count on some type of pool or tub. Despite their remote location, Turkey Creek Hot Springs is rather well known, so don't expect to have the area to yourself.

I recommend making this trip in the late summer or early fall. Other times can be treacherous, with high water levels and flash floods. Be sure to contact the Gila National Forest for road and trail conditions (Silver City Ranger District: 505-538-2771. I also recommend that you backpack this trip, instead of trying to do it in one day. You may find yourself frustrated by not having enough time. The 4-mile distance is deceiving—the hike takes much longer due to frequent river and creek crossings. Be sure to let someone know when and where you are going and when you expect to be back.

15

Mangas Warm Springs

General description: A series of warm-water seeps alongside U.S. Highway 180. No bathing opportunities.

Location: Southwestern New Mexico, in the small town of Mangas, immediately off US 180.

Primitive/developed: Primitive. The springs themselves have not been altered, although the hot water is used to irrigate grazing fields at a nearby ranch.

Best time of year: Year-round.

Restrictions: The springs are adjacent to private property. Be sure to obey all "No Trespassing" signs.

Access: The springs can be reached by any vehicle, because they are located immediately off US 180.

Water temperature: The source is about 81 degrees F.

Mangas Warm Springs

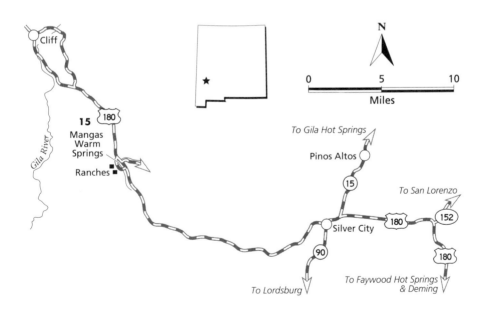

Nearby attractions: Turkey Creek Hot Springs, San Francisco Hot Springs, Bubbles Hot Springs.
Services: Gas, food, and lodging can all be found in Silver City, about 20 miles to the southeast.
Camping: No camping is permitted at Mangas.
Map: USGS Silver City, New Mexico quadrangle (1:100,000 scale).

Finding the spring: From Silver City, head northwest on US 180 for about 20 miles to the small town of Mangas. A narrow paved road on your left (west) parallels the highway. Follow this road as it passes by several warm-water seeps along the base of the highway.

The hot springs: The springs are characterized by lush vegetation and several small pools of water. The water flows over and under the road to irrigate large grazing fields at a nearby ranch. Mangas Warm Springs is another example of the great variety of geothermal resources in this part of the state. Although Mangas does not provide bathing opportunities, it is a pleasant diversion if you are headed in either direction on US 180 northwest of Silver City. Be sure to obey all private property and "No Trespassing" signs.

TRUTH OR CONSEQUENCES

The town of Truth or Consequences is unique in many ways. Although its original name was Hot Springs (for obvious reasons), the town agreed to change its name in the 1950s after the popular television show.

Prehistorically, the hot springs were revered by both the Mimbres Indians as well as the later arriving Apache. Geronimo was said to have spent considerable time enjoying the springs. The Spanish called the springs Ojo Caliente de Las Palomas (Hot Springs of the Doves). During the nineteenth century, farmers and ranchers used the hot springs for bathing, although they were undeveloped. When the construction of Elephant Butte Dam began in 1911, many workers came to the area that is now Truth or Consequences. To service these workers, bars and dance halls emerged near the dam site at a town that became known as Palomas Hot Springs. Soon thereafter, Palomas was dropped from the name. During the 1930s, hot-spring establishments began to emerge in the town. Because of the Depression, these facilities were necessarily simple resorts. At its height, the town contained 12 hot-spring resorts and hotels. Today the town is known for its no-frills hot-spring resorts and fishing and boating opportunities on the nearby Elephant Butte Reservoir. It is also well known as a unique stop along Interstate 25. Many of the resorts have fallen into disrepair in the past couple decades, although some have been recently renovated. The best time of year to enjoy TorC is generally in the winter, late fall, or early spring. Summers can be very hot. Below are most of the hot bath establishments open as of summer 1999. For more information, call each establishment, or call the TorC Chamber of Commerce at 505-894-3536.

Plenty of relaxing, healing waters are available at Truth or Consequences.

16

Riverbend Hot Springs

General description: A unique and interesting combination of youth hostel and hot mineral bath establishment.

Location: Southern New Mexico, in the town of Truth or Consequences.

Primitive/developed: Developed. However, the resort and hostel are definitely no-frills and have a very rustic charm.

Best time of year: Year-round, although summers can be hot.

Restrictions: This private establishment is open to visitors and guests.

Access: Easy access, in town.

Water temperature: The hot water is brought up from a well at about 114 degrees F, but cools off to about 108 degrees F in the tubs.

Nearby attractions: Elephant Butte Reservoir, other hot springs in Truth or Consequences.

Services: Gas, food, and lodging can be found in Truth or Consequences, and either private or dormitory-style rooms can be rented at Riverbend.

Camping: Camping is permitted at Riverbend; call for rates. Ample camping opportunities are also available at nearby Elephant Butte Lake State Park.

Map: New Mexico State Highway Map.

Facilities at Riverbend Hot Springs.

Truth or Consequences Resorts

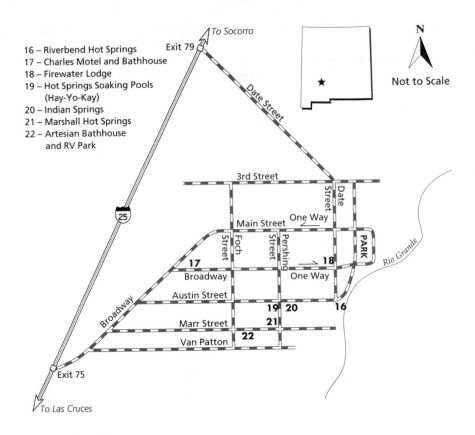

16 – Riverbend Hot Springs
17 – Charles Motel and Bathhouse
18 – Firewater Lodge
19 – Hot Springs Soaking Pools
    (Hay-Yo-Kay)
20 – Indian Springs
21 – Marshall Hot Springs
22 – Artesian Bathhouse
    and RV Park

Not to Scale

Finding the spring: From Interstate 25 traveling north, take exit 75 and continue toward downtown TorC. Follow Broadway to Austin Avenue, then turn right. Follow Austin to Riverbend Hot Springs on your right. From I-25 traveling south, take exit 79 and follow the road for 1.5 miles to Date Street. Follow Date as it turns into Main, and turn left on Pershing. Follow Pershing across Broadway then turn left on Austin. Follow Austin to Riverbend.

The hot springs: Riverbend is one of the better mineral bath establishments in town. It is located immediately adjacent to the Rio Grande, allowing for a cold plunge in between baths. Riverbend is designed around a youth hostel, which offers dormitory-style lodging (bunk beds in separate men's and women's rooms) or private rooms. The accommodations all share bathrooms as well as a kitchen and living room. The hot mineral water is drawn from the ground and pumped into three large tubs overlooking the river. The tubs were originally used as bait tanks by the previous owner. The owners generally fill the tubs twice a day with fresh water, once in the morning and once in the evening, for guests of the hostel. They will, however, fill the tubs for visitors for $5. For further information, call Riverbend at 505-894-6183, visit them online at www.riolink.com/~rivrbnd, or e-mail them at rivrbnd@riolink.com.

17
Charles Motel and Bathhouse

(See map on page 52)

General description: A historic motel and hot mineral bath establishment that offers several private mineral baths.
Location: Southern New Mexico, in the town of Truth or Consequences.
Primitive/developed: Developed. However, the motel and bathhouse are definitely no-frills and have a very rustic charm.
Best time of year: Year-round, although summers can be hot.
Restrictions: This private establishment is open to visitors and guests.
Access: Easy access, in town.
Water temperature: The hot water is brought up from a well at about 114 degrees F. Bath temperatures vary from 98 to 108 degrees F.
Nearby attractions: Elephant Butte Reservoir, other hot springs in Truth or Consequences.
Services: Gas, food, and lodging can be found in Truth or Consequences. Rooms are available at Charles.
Camping: Camping is not permitted at Charles, but plenty of campsites are available at nearby Elephant Butte Lake State Park.
Map: New Mexico State Highway Map.

Finding the spring: From Interstate 25 traveling north, take exit 75 and continue toward downtown Truth or Consequences. Follow Broadway east for a few blocks to Clancy Street. Charles is located on the corner of these two streets at 601 Broadway.

The hot springs: Charles is one of the oldest bathing facilities in Truth or Consequences. Established in the 1930s by Charles Lockhart, the motel and bathhouse have not changed much since. The bathhouse contains nine tubs, all relatively new ceramic and tile. The bathhouse is divided into men's and women's sides, although couples can share a single tub. Hot water is drawn from depth and can be mixed with cold water to create the ideal bath temperature, depending upon the taste of the bather. Massage and reflexology are also available. The bathhouse is generally open between 8 A.M. and 9 P.M. every day. Phone 505-894-7154 for current rates or reservations at the motel.

18

Firewater Lodge

(See map on page 52)

General description: A combination bathhouse and motel that was recently renovated and contains new baths and facilities.
Location: Southern New Mexico, in the town of Truth or Consequences.
Primitive/developed: Developed. However, the motel and bathhouse are definitely no-frills.
Best time of year: Year-round, although summers can be hot.
Restrictions: This private establishment is open to visitors and guests.
Access: Easy access, in town.
Water temperature: The hot water is brought up from the ground at about 112 degrees F, and ranges between 106 and 110 degrees F in the tubs.
Nearby attractions: Elephant Butte Reservoir, other hot springs in Truth or Consequences.
Services: Gas, food, and lodging can be found in Truth or Consequences. Very small, spartan rooms are available at the Firewater Lodge.
Camping: Camping is not premitted at Firewater, but plenty of camp-sites are available at nearby Elephant Butte Lake State Park.
Map: New Mexico State Highway Map.

Finding the spring: From Interstate 25 traveling north, take exit 75 and continue toward downtown Truth or Consequences. Follow Broadway east a few blocks to Firewater Lodge, at 309 Broadway.

The hot springs: Firewater Lodge contains several tubs in private rooms. The hot water is drawn from the ground, where it flows near the surface. The tubs have recently been renovated and are made of concrete and tile. There are a few spartan rooms available at the bathhouse. Phone 505-894-3405 for current rates or reservations.

19

Hot Springs Soaking Pools (Hay-Yo-Kay)

(See map on page 52)

General description: A simple, historic bathhouse with three individual tubs and two larger pools.
Location: Southern New Mexico, in the town of Truth or Consequences.
Primitive/developed: Developed, although a no-frills establishment.
Best time of year: Year-round, although summers can be hot.
Restrictions: This private establishment is open to visitors.
Access: Easy access, in town.
Water temperature: The hot water is brought up from the ground at about 110 degrees F, and ranges between 104 and 108 degrees F in the tubs and pools.
Nearby attractions: Elephant Butte Reservoir, other hot springs in Truth or Consequences.
Services: Gas, food, and lodging can be found in Truth or Consequences.
Camping: Camping is not permitted at Hot Springs Soaking Pools but plenty of campsites are available at nearby Elephant Butte Lake State Park.
Map: New Mexico State Highway Map.

Finding the spring: From Interstate 25 traveling north, take exit 75 and continue toward downtown Truth or Consequences. Follow Broadway east for a few blocks to Pershing Street, then turn right. Follow Pershing to Austin Avenue. Hot Springs Soaking Pools is located at the corner of Austin and Pershing, at 300 Austin.

The hot springs: Previously known as Hay-Yo-Kay, this is the oldest continuously operating bathhouse in town, having opened in the 1930s. Hot Springs Soaking Pools is similar to Indian Springs in many ways. The hot water is drawn from a hot ditch just below the surface, then diverted into three private tubs and two larger pools. The baths and pools contain sand and rock bottoms. All the pools can be rented for individual, private use. The bathhouse is generally open Monday, Tuesday, Thursday, and Friday from 9 A.M. to noon and from 3 to 7 P.M., and on Saturday and Sunday from noon to 7 P.M. Phone 505-894-2228 for current rates or reserations.

20

Indian Springs

(See map on page 52)

General description: A no-frills hot bath establishment that contains one natural bath and limited accommodations.
Location: Southern New Mexico, in the town of Truth or Consequences.
Primitive/developed: Developed. However, the motel and bathhouse are definitely no-frills.
Best time of year: Year-round, although summers can be hot.
Restrictions: This private establishment is open to visitors and guests.
Access: Easy access, in town
Water temperature: The hot water is brought up from the ground at about 110 degrees F, and is about 106 degrees F in the bath itself.
Nearby attractions: Elephant Butte Reservoir, other hot springs in Truth or Consequences.
Services: Gas, food, and lodging can be found in Truth or Consequences. Very small, spartan rooms are available at Indian Springs.
Camping: Camping is not permitted at Indian Springs, but there are plenty of campsites at nearby Elephant Butte Lake State Park.
Map: New Mexico State Highway Map.

Finding the spring: From Interstate 25 traveling north, take exit 75 and continue toward downtown Truth or Consequences. Follow Broadway east for a few blocks to Pershing Street, then turn right. Follow Pershing to Austin Avenue, then turn left. Indian Springs is located at 218 Austin.

The hot springs: Indian Springs consists of one small pool enclosed by a small bathhouse. The hot water is drawn from the ground, where it flows near the surface. The bath itself is a sand- and rock-bottomed pool, with a temperature of about 106 degrees F. There are a few rooms available at the bathhouse, although they are very small. Do not expect to be pampered here. Phone 505-894-2018 for current rates or reservations.

21

Marshall Hot Springs

(See map on page 52)

General description: A small bathhouse with three pools fed by natural hot-spring water.

Location: Southern New Mexico, in the town of Truth or Consequences.

Primitive/developed: Developed, However, the bathhouse is definitely no-frills.

Best time of year: Year-round, although summers can be hot.

Restrictions: This private establishment is open to visitors.

Access: Easy access, in town.

Water temperature: The hot water is brought up from the ground at about 110 degrees F, and ranges between 104 and 108 degrees F in the various tubs.

Nearby attractions: Elephant Butte Reservoir, other hot springs in Truth or Consequences.

Services: Gas, food, and lodging can be found in Truth or Consequences.

Camping: Camping is not permitted at Marshall, but plenty of campsites are available at nearby Elephant Butte Lake State Park.

Map: New Mexico State Highway Map.

Finding the spring: From Interstate 25 traveling north, take exit 75 and continue toward downtown Truth or Consequences. Follow Broadway east for a few blocks to Pershing Street, then turn right. Follow Pershing for 2 blocks to Marr Avenue. Marshall is located at 311 Marr.

The hot springs: Like many of the other bathhouses in Truth or Consequences, Marshall consists of a small bathhouse with three private pools. The hot water is drawn from the ground into the sand- and rock-bottomed pools, with temperatures ranging from 104 to 108 degrees F. The pools can be rented for private use. The pools are deeper than most in town; Marshall also tends to have a more New Age feel to it, complete with incense and music, if you like. Phone 505-894-9286 for current rates or reservations.

22

Artesian Bathhouse and RV Park

(See map on page 52)

General description: A small bathhouse complete with eight tubs and an RV park.

Location: Southern New Mexico, in the town of Truth or Consequences.

Primitive/developed: Developed. However, the bathhouse is definitely no-frills.

Best time of year: Year-round, although summers can be hot.

Restrictions: This private establishment is open to guests and visitors.

Access: Easy access, in town.

Water temperature: The hot water is brought up from the ground from an artesian well at about 112 degrees F; temperatures range between 98 and 108 degrees F in the various tubs.

Nearby attractions: Elephant Butte Reservoir, other hot springs in Truth or Consequences.

Services: Gas, food, and lodging can be found in Truth or Consequences.

Camping: RV camping is available at Artesian by the day, week, or month. Plenty of campsites also are available at nearby Elephant Butte Lake State Park.

Map: New Mexico State Highway Map.

Finding the spring: From Interstate 25 traveling north, take exit 75 and continue toward downtown TorC. Follow Broadway east to Foch Street, then turn right. Follow Foch for 2 blocks to Marr Avenue, then turn left. Artesian is located at 312 Marr.

The hot springs: Artesian is small and unassuming, like the other facilities in Truth or Consequences. The hot water is drawn from the only artesian well in town and diverted into eight baths. There are five individual tubs and three larger baths for two or more people. Pool temperatures range from 98 to 108 degrees F. The bathhouse is open daily from 8 A.M. to 6 P.M., except Wednesday. Phone 505-894-2684 for current rates or reservations.

Socorro

Like other New Mexican towns, Socorro attracted Europeans who came to the area to establish a mission in the early 1600s. San Miguel was founded in 1620, but was destroyed in the Pueblo Revolt of 1680. It was later rebuilt in the early 1800s, and has been in continual use since then. Visitors are welcome to the historic site, which is located at 403 Camino Real (just north of the plaza).

Following the discovery of silver in nearby mountains, the rough mining town of Socorro developed in the late 1870s and into the 1880s and became the most notorious city in New Mexico. Like other mining towns, Socorro had its share of violence, rapid accumulation of wealth, and general excitement. With the rush of hopeful settlers, the town was the largest in the territory for a time. However, the Panic of 1893 caused silver prices to drop and local mines reacted by producing zinc. After the depletion of these ores, the town began to decline.

Eventually the town was reborn as a center for farmers and ranchers, as well as a supply center for passing travelers.

23

Sedillo Springs

General description: A collection of small hot springs in a beautiful setting outside the town of Socorro. Sedillo currently does not offer bathing opportunities, but this may change.
Location: Central New Mexico, about 3 miles northwest of Socorro.
Primitive/developed: Primitive. The springs are currently undeveloped, but at one time there were several tubs and a large pool.
Best time of year: Fall, winter, and spring. Summer is too hot.
Restrictions: Be sure to obey all posted signs.
Access: The resort can be reached via a graded dirt road and a short hike.
Water temperature: The source is about 93 degrees F.
Nearby attractions: Cibola National Forest.
Services: Gas, food, and lodging are available in Socorro, a short drive from the springs.
Camping: Camping is likely not permitted at the springs. Countless opportunities for undeveloped camping are available in nearby Cibola National Forest, however.
Map: USGS Socorro, New Mexico quadrangle (1:100,000 scale).

Sedillo Springs

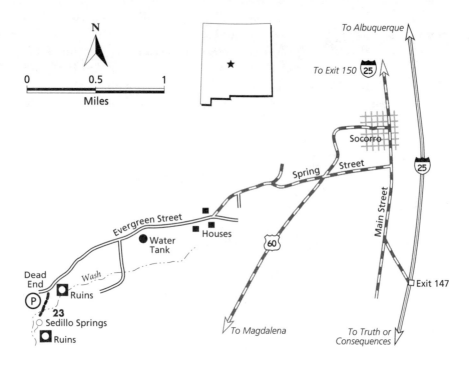

Finding the spring: From Interstate 25, take exit 147 at the town of Socorro. Travel north on Main Street to Spring Street, where you turn (left) west. Cross U.S. Highway 60 and travel about 1 mile to Evergreen Street, then turn left. Stay on the paved road as it curves around to the right, and continue on this road until the pavement ends. Take the dirt road to your right (passing a house on your left) and immediately bear left on the main dirt road. Continue on this good graded dirt road past a road leading to the water tank on your left. Continue 0.25 mile more to where the road ends. Park here and follow a faint trail off to your left. You will see the ruins of adobe buildings in the area. Walk for 0.25 mile, crossing into and out of a wash, to a collection of cottonwood trees and other vegetation. The springs are in the collection of greenery.

The hot springs: Sedillo Springs consists of a small group of warm springs with low flows. The water comes out of the ground at about 93 degrees F and is directed downhill, passing several old tubs. It then reaches a large reservoir that may have been a pool at one time, but the tubs and reservoir are all empty now, and the site appears to be used only by nighttime party-types. There really are no bathing opportunities here, but there may be in the future. Please obey all signs and respect the area by not leaving trash behind.

Several adobe buildings attest to the presence of a small settlement in the vicinity of Sedillo Springs in the past. Little remains to indicate what was here, however. There are several other hot and warm springs in the vicinity of Socorro, but most of them are on private property and are not open to the general public.

Northern New Mexico Hot Springs

Jemez Springs Area (Santa Fe National Forest)

The Santa Fe National Forest is blessed with countless hot and warm springs. The area around Jemez Springs is particularly rich in geothermal resources. For hot-spring enthusiasts in New Mexico, this is one of the best areas for the natural experience. Although many of the hot springs are privately owned, plenty are on national forest land and are open to public use. Many of the springs listed below require hiking to reach them. Although this does provide for a more rustic experience, most of the springs are rather well known, and one can expect to be sharing the experience with others.

The Santa Fe National Forest presents beautiful scenery as well as a multitude of outdoor activities such as fishing, hiking, camping, and backpacking. The area is serviced by the small hamlet of Jemez Springs, as well as the larger town of Los Alamos to the west. Before visiting the springs in the area, be sure to contact the Santa Fe National Forest for weather, access, and other information. The Jemez Ranger District, which encompasses most of the springs listed here, can be reached at 505-829-3535.

24

Spence Hot Springs

General description: A collection of natural hot springs on the side of a steep hill, forming several soaking pools. Heavily visited, Spence has had a reputation as a hangout for nudists.

Location: Northern New Mexico, in the Santa Fe National Forest, about 32 miles west of Los Alamos.

Primitive/developed: Primitive. The only improvement has been the construction of several rock pools. Otherwise, the springs are in a pristine state.

Best time of year: Spring, summer, and fall. Roads may be closed in winter.

Spence Hot Springs

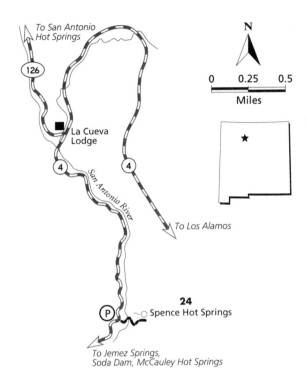

Restrictions: The USDA Forest Service manages the springs; be sure to obey all posted rules. Currently, access parking is permitted only during daylight hours.

Access: The springs are located a short hike off New Mexico Highway 4.

Water temperature: The source is about 100 degrees F, and the pools are slightly cooler.

Nearby attractions: The surrounding Santa Fe National Forest offers a multitude of attractions. Several other hot springs are located in the vicinity, including Jemez Springs, Soda Dam, and San Antonio.

Services: Gas, food, and lodging can be found in Los Alamos, about 32 miles to the east.

Camping: Camping is not permitted at Spence, even in the parking lot. There are several Forest Service campgrounds in the area, however.

Map: USGS Los Alamos, New Mexico quadrangle (1:100,000 scale).

Spence Hot Springs.

Finding the spring: From Los Alamos, travel west on NM 4 for about 30 miles to NM 126 at La Cueva Lodge. Continue on NM 4 for another 1.5 miles and park in the large parking area on your left. As you face the river, look for a well-worn path down to the right at the end of the parking lot. The short trail takes you across the San Antonio River and up the hillside to the springs. There are two sets of springs to enjoy, one lower and one upper.

The hot springs: A very popular set of hot springs, Spence usually has several people partaking. The water is about 100 degrees F, so it's not extremely hot, but it is invigorating nonetheless. A small waterfall can even be found in the lower springs, which also may contain up to three other pools, depending upon how the water has been diverted. From the lower pools you can continue uphill, following the water and a small trail. Several other pools are located alongside the small creek formed by the hot-spring water. All of the pools are fantastic and set in a beautiful location. They are easy to reach, hence the large number of visitors.

Spence has had a long and varied history. For years it was a favorite hangout for nudists. Following some unsavory conduct and several complaints, the Forest Service attempted to regulate the springs to a greater degree. As a result, visitation is permitted only during daylight hours. Although officially the Forest Service has prohibited nudity, it has been for the most part allowed to continue. Do not be surprised to find that this is the prevailing mode of bathing at Spence. It is rare to have the area to yourself, so if you are seeking solitude and peace, you might want to try another spring nearby, such as San Antonio or McCauley.

Please help to keep this location open by obeying posted signs and not littering. If problems persist at Spence, there is a chance that the Forest Service will close all public access, which would be a shame.

25

McCauley Hot Springs

General description: A collection of spectacular natural hot springs in the Jemez Springs area, with several large pools of warm water perfect for bathing.

Location: Northern New Mexico, in the Santa Fe National Forest, about 35 miles west of Los Alamos.

Primitive/developed: Primitive. The only alteration has been the construction of several rock dams, which created pools for bathing.

Best time of year: Late spring, summer, and early fall. The trails can be virtually impassable in early spring and winter. Roads may also be closed in winter.

Restrictions: The springs are in the Santa Fe National Forest; be sure to obey all USDA Forest Service regulations.

Access: A hike of about 2 miles is required to reach the springs. During high river levels, this trail may be difficult or even impassable.

Water temperature: The source is about 100 degrees F. The water cools as it flows downhill into the various pools.

Nearby attractions: Spence Hot Springs, San Antonio Hot Springs, Jemez Springs.

Services: Gas, food, and lodging can be found in Los Alamos, about 35 miles to the east. Jemez Springs offers a store, restaurant, and lodge.

Camping: Undeveloped camping is permitted at the spring, but you must pack in everything you need. Several Forest Service campgrounds are located in the area, too.

Maps: USGS Los Alamos, New Mexico quadrangle (1:100,000 scale); Jemez Springs and Redondo Peak, New Mexico quadrangles (1:24,000 scale).

Finding the spring: From Los Alamos, travel west on New Mexico Highway 4 for about 30 miles to NM 126 at La Cueva Lodge. Continue on NM 4 for

McCauley Hot Springs

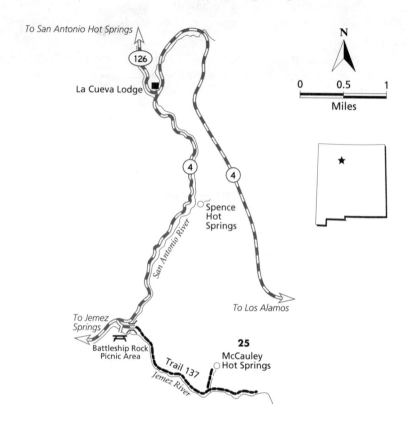

another 2 miles to the Battleship Rock Picnic Area (past the parking area for Spence Hot Springs). Pull into the picnic area and park. Cross the bridge to the large gazebo in the fireplace area. Behind the gazebo is the trailhead for the East Fork Trail, or Trail 137. Follow this trail as it winds its way along the Jemez River. During periods of higher water, you may find yourself going up the hillside and back down again to avoid the river. Hike for 1.75 miles until you see a small stream flowing downhill on your left. This is water from McCauley Hot Springs. Follow this small creek because there is no well-defined trail. Hike uphill for about a quater of a mile until you reach several pools of water. The top and largest pool is the source.

The hot springs: A fabulous collection of hot springs, McCauley is well worth the 2-mile hike to reach it. The source bubbles out of the ground on a relatively steep hillside and flows into a large pond with crystal-clear water. From here the water flows downhill into many other pools, each slightly

McCauley Hot Springs, first pool.

cooler than the previous one. Small dams have been constructed to capture this water in pools. The scenery is fantastic. Despite the sometimes difficult hike along the Jemez River, do not expect to have McCauley to yourself. It is a well-known and well-publicized collection of springs. Both bathing suits and nudity are common at the springs. Be sure to hike only during low-flow periods of the Jemez River. The river is impassable during the late fall, winter, and early part of spring.

26

San Antonio Hot Springs

General description: A fabulous collection of hot springs flowing out of a steep hillside and forming several usable pools.

Location: Northern New Mexico, in the Santa Fe National Forest, about 40 miles west of Los Alamos.

Primitive/developed: Primitive. The only improvement has been the formation of several rock-lined pools.

Best time of year: Late spring, summer, and early fall. Roads are closed in winter.

Relaxing at San Antonio Hot Springs.

Restrictions: The springs are located on national forest land, and all USDA Forest Service regulations must be obeyed.

Access: A 5-mile hike, bike, or horseback ride, which includes climbing a steep hill, is required to reach the springs.

Water temperature: The source is about 129 degrees F. The water cools substantially as it flows downhill into the various pools; the top one is about 105 degrees F.

Nearby attractions: Spence Hot Springs, McCauley Hot Springs, Jemez Springs.

Services: Gas, food, and lodging can be found in Los Alamos, about 40 miles to the east. Jemez Springs offers a store, restaurant, and lodge.

Camping: Undeveloped camping is permitted in the area near the springs, although certain areas are off-limits. Several developed campgrounds are available in the area, also.

Map: USGS 7 Springs, New Mexico quadrangle (1:24,000 scale).

Finding the spring: From Los Alamos, travel west on New Mexico Highway 4 for about 30 miles to NM 126 at La Cueva Lodge. Turn right on NM 126 and drive for about 3.7 miles to Forest Service Road 376 on your right. Turn here and park at the gate. The road is closed to motor vehicles. The only way to reach the springs is by hiking, biking, or horseback riding. Follow the road as it goes through the forest for 5 miles until you reach what looks to be an

San Antonio Hot Springs

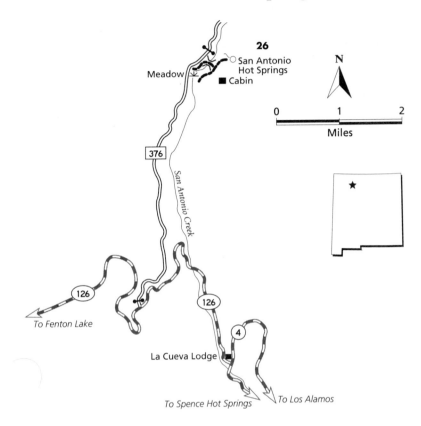

intersection and a large cabin across the San Antonio Creek to your right. Take the road to the right as it goes downhill and then crosses the creek at a small bridge. Follow a faint trail up the steep hillside. You will see water from the hot springs flowing down the hill. The walk up the hill to the springs is less than 0.25 mile, but it is steep.

The hot springs: In a magnificent setting, San Antonio is a must-visit if you are in the Santa Fe National Forest, Jemez Springs area. Although it's a 5-mile trek to get there, the springs are well worth it. Flowing out of a steep hillside, the water comes out of the ground at about 129 degrees F and forms the first of several pools. The springs' source was actually bolstered by the Civilian Conservation Corps (CCC) in the 1930s to ensure a regular flow. The top pool is large and shallow, and is perfect if you want a hot soak. The water then flows downhill into several smaller pools, each one successively cooler. No matter which one you pick, you will have a great view of the surrounding valley, creek, and forest. Despite the journey required to reach the springs, you can generally expect to find others at this spot. Bathing suits and nudity are common at San Antonio Hot Springs. Be sure to leave plenty of time to hike in and out, and bring plenty of drinking water.

Like Spence Hot Springs, the Forest Service has had problems with San Antonio. Vandalism to the nearby CCC cabin has caused the Forest Service to limit access. Please respect the cabin and the hot springs and do not damage either, ensuring that the area will stay open to the public.

27

Soda Dam

(See map on page 73)

General description: A magnificent natural dam formed in the Jemez River by the precipitation of minerals from a collection of hot springs. Although no bathing opportunities are available, the dam is located immediately off the main highway and is well worth a stop.

Location: Northern New Mexico, 2 miles north of Jemez Springs and about 35 miles west of Los Alamos.

Primitive/developed: Primitive. No improvements have been made to the springs. Portions of the original natural dam were blown up for the construction of the highway.

Best time of year: Late spring, summer, and early fall. Some roads may be closed during winter.

Restrictions: The dam is only open for daytime use. Be careful near the edge of the river as ledges can be slippery and steep.

Access: Soda Dam is located immediately off New Mexico Highway 4.

Water temperature: The source is about 117 degrees F.

Nearby attractions: Spence Hot Springs, McCauley Hot Springs, Jemez Springs. The Santa Fe National Forest also offers almost unlimited outdoor recreation, including hiking, camping, backpacking, and fishing.

Services: Gas, food, and lodging can be found in Los Alamos, about 40 miles to the east. The small town of Jemez Springs offers a store, restaurant, and lodge.

Camping: Camping is not permitted at Soda Dam. Several developed campgrounds are located in the surrounding Santa Fe National Forest, as well as on the Jemez River south along NM 4.

Map: USGS Los Alamos, New Mexico quadrangle (1:100,000 scale).

Exploring Soda Dam.

Finding the spring: From Los Alamos, travel west on NM 4 for about 30 miles to NM 126 at La Cueva Lodge. Continue on NM 4 for another 6 miles until you reach Soda Dam on your left (east). There is a USDA Forest Service sign immediately before the springs. If you reach the town of Jemez Springs, you have gone 1 mile too far.

The hot springs: A fantastic geologic wonder, Soda Dam was created over hundreds of years by hot mineral water flow. The hot springs precipitated minerals (including calcium carbonate) that eventually formed a dam across the Jemez River, constricting the river's flow. During the construction of NM 4, a portion of the dam was removed. However, the most dramatic section remains, immediately to the east of the highway, where the river rushes through a small opening in the mineral precipitate. Small caves have been constructed by the springs, making for a very interesting site. Rock shelters can be found in the immediate vicinity of Soda Dam, including the famous Jemez Cave. An extensive archaeological deposit was found in the cave during the 1930s, indicating that the area around Soda Dam has been used for more than 2,000 years by a variety of cultures. It is small wonder when you consider the abundant cold and warm water found at this beautiful location. A variety of hot-spring sources exist in the area of Soda Dam, including several small seeps, which can be found in the small cave adjacent to the dam. You can see some other hot springs immediately across the road from Soda Dam, but these are little more than puddles of warm water, running along the highway for a short distance. A pullout and parking area and an interpretive sign are the only development around the springs. There are no bathing opportunities here, but it's definitely worth a stop when driving along NM 4. Take a few minutes to explore and enjoy this geologic wonder.

28

Jemez Springs Bathhouse

General description: A historic hot mineral bathhouse that still offers baths in the old-fashioned way. Located at the margin of the Santa Fe National Forest, the bathhouse is in an irresistible setting.

Location: Northern New Mexico, in the small town of Jemez Springs. Jemez Springs is located between the Santa Fe National Forest and the Jemez Indian Reservation, about 37 miles west of Los Alamos and 17 miles north of the small town of San Ysidro.

Primitive/developed: Developed. However, the bathhouse still possesses a rustic charm.

Best time of year: Year-round.

Restrictions: This private establishment is open to visitors.

Access: The resort is located immediately off New Mexico Highway 4.

Water temperature: The source is about169 degrees F. Bath temperatures can be regulated with cold water.

Nearby attractions: Jemez State Monument, Soda Dam, Spence Hot Springs, and McCauley Hot Springs.

Services: Gas, food, and lodging can be found in Los Alamos, about 37 miles to the east. Jemez Springs offers a store, restaurant, and lodge.

Camping: Camping is not permitted at Jemez Springs Bathhouse. Several developed campgrounds are located in the Santa Fe National Forest, as well as on the Jemez River south along NM 4.

Map: New Mexico State Highway Map

Finding the spring: From Los Alamos, travel west on NM 4 for about 30 miles to NM 126 at La Cueva Lodge. Continue on NM 4 for about 7 miles (passing Soda Dam) to the town of Jemez Springs. The bathhouse is hard to miss in town. From San Ysidro, travel north on NM 4 for about 20 miles to the town of Jemez Springs.

Soda Dam, Jemez Springs Bathhouse

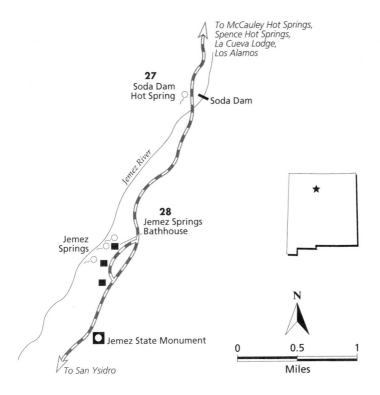

To McCauley Hot Springs,
Spence Hot Springs,
La Cueva Lodge,
Los Alamos

27
Soda Dam
Hot Spring

Soda Dam

Jemez River

28
Jemez Springs
Bathhouse

Jemez
Springs

Jemez State Monument

To San Ysidro

N

0   0.5   1

Miles

The hot springs: Located in an incredibly rich geothermal area, Jemez Springs were named for the hot springs from which the bathhouse gets its water. According to locals, in 1860 settlers heard a roar and then witnessed the hot springs erupt like a geyser. Following the eruption, a rock enclosure was constructed around the hot springs, and the water has been used ever since. The bathhouse was constructed sometime in the 1870s and is one of the oldest buildings in the area. It has not been changed much since that time.

Puebloan peoples have been living along the Jemez River for centuries, undoubtedly using the plentiful hot springs of the area. Spanish explorers and missionaries first in the sixteenth century. Franciscan missionaries built a stone church, named San Jose de Guisewa, in 1622, in an attempt to Christianize the local Native Americans. A small group of Jemez Indians was already living in a community called Guisewa, which means "place at the boiling waters." Today a state monument marks the place where the Jemez people built their homes. The Spanish, however, forced the Puebloans to settle farther

Jemez Springs bathhouse.

down the valley, in the location of the present-day reservation. During the 1840s, when whites first began to settle in the area, a town called Ojos Calientes emerged around the hot springs. In 1888 the town's name was changed to Archuleta, after the family who had built the first bathhouse at the spring in the previous decade. Finally, in 1907 the town's name was changed to Jemez Springs. At the height of the popularity of hot-spring resorts, there were two in Jemez Springs, including the one you see today. In the 1940s and 1950s, the current bathhouse was used by the Catholic Church as a retreat for priests. In 1961, the property was sold to the town of Jemez Springs, in whose hands it remains today. The bathhouse is leased to a group of individuals who operate it.

You can choose from private outdoor or private individual indoor tubs. The tubs are old-fashioned bathtubs, and the hot mineral water is fed directly into them. Because the source water is so hot (169 degrees F), cold water must be added to find the right temperature. This is left up to you to find your ideal mix. The indoor tubs are for individual use, while the outdoor cedar tub can fit up to six people. Prices as of 1999 were $8 for half an hour and $12 for 1 hour; the outdoor cedar tub is $30 for 1 hour. Massages range from $30 for half an hour to $62 for 1.5 hours. Hot showers are $3, and towel and suit rental is $1. Generally, you do not have to phone ahead for reservations, except during peak visitation hours on summer weekends. Do phone ahead for massages and the outdoor tub. Summer hours are from 9 A.M. to 9 P.M., and winter hours are from 10 A.M. to 7:30 P.M. The bathhouse is open seven days a week.

Several other hot springs exist in the area, including one used by a Buddhist center, adjacent to the Jemez Springs Bathhouse. The original Jemez Hot Springs are located immediately behind the bathhouse in a covered gazebo. Other hot springs can be found adjacent to the Jemez River, although none provide bathing opportunities.

SANTA FE AREA

The tourist capital of the state, Santa Fe provides ample opportunities to experience New Mexico's rich cultural and recreational resources. Founded in 1607, Santa Fe is one of the oldest occupied cities in North America. Its long tradition of Native American, Spanish, Mexican, and Anglo roots gives it a distinctive flavor and feel. The original plaza is still in place, surrounded by art galleries, restaurants, and shops. The town has been able to maintain its connection to the past despite its growth and popularity. Be sure to visit the Palace of the Governors. Constructed in the seventeenth century by the Spanish, the palace dominated the plaza (and still does). The building withstood the violent revolt of the Pueblo Indians in 1680 and has served as the seat of power for New Spain, Mexico, the Confederate States of America, and the United States. Today the building houses a fantastic museum representing New Mexico's history.

Santa Fe also serves as the gateway to much of New Mexico's wilderness areas. The Sangre de Cristo Mountains are a short drive to the east and offer ample opportunities for hiking, biking, backpacking, camping, fishing, and skiing. Although there are virtually no natural hot springs in the immediate Santa Fe area, the Japanese-style Ten Thousand Waves spa offers plenty of hot-water alternatives, and is only a short drive into the mountains north of Santa Fe.

29

Ten Thousand Waves

General description: A Japanese-style hot mineral water health spa that offers an incredible variety of treatments and bathing options.
Location: Northern New Mexico, a few miles outside Santa Fe.
Primitive/developed: Developed. There are actually no natural hot springs at Ten Thousand Waves, but visitors are offered a wide assortment of features and amenities.
Best time of year: Year-round.
Restrictions: This is a private establishment; be sure to obey all posted rules.
Access: The resort is located a few miles up a paved road from Santa Fe.
Water temperature: The well water is heated by use of a gas heater and purified before reaching the tubs, which range in temperature between 97 and 106 degrees F.

Ten Thousand Waves

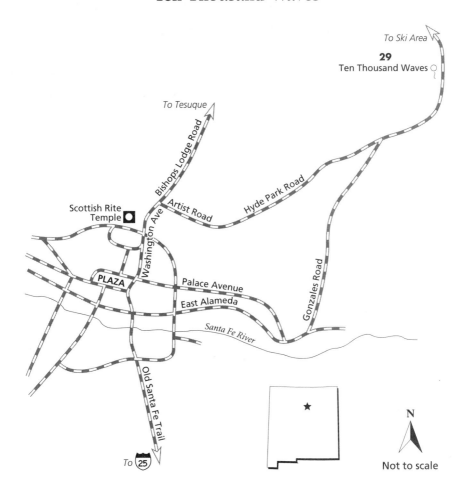

Nearby attractions: Town of Santa Fe, Hyde Memorial State Park, Santa Fe Ski Area.

Services: Gas, food, and lodging can be found in Santa Fe, less than 4 miles away. Lodging is available at Ten Thousand Waves, with a choice of eight different suites ranging in price from $125 to $205 per night.

Camping: Camping is not permitted at Ten Thousand Waves, but is available in the nearby Santa Fe National Forest.

Map: Santa Fe area map.

Ten Thousand Waves. Photo courtesy of Ten Thousand Waves.

Finding the spring: From the plaza in downtown Santa Fe, follow Washington Avenue north, past the Scottish Rite Temple to Artist Road. Turn right on Artist Road and follow it as it turns into Hyde Park Road, with signs for the ski area. Stay on Hyde Park Road for about 3 miles to Ten Thousand Waves on your left.

The hot springs: Although just a short drive outside Santa Fe, Ten Thousand Waves is far enough away to give one the sense of seclusion. With nine tubs to choose from and a variety of massage options, spa treatments, facial and skin care treatments, and a new Japanese hot stone massage treatment, you could spend days here. Upon entering the main building, you are given a locker for personal belongings and a kimono for wearing around the grounds. Following a shower, there are several bathing opportunities.

Two communal tubs are located outside, one for men and women, and another for women only. One indoor tub accommodates up to ten people and contains a bathroom, cooling area, and sauna. The rest of the outdoor tubs are either wooden or acrylic, and they're secluded enough from each other to provide privacy. There is also a warm waterfall complete with warm tub, rock deck, steam room, and cold plunge. The treatments are too numerous to mention here, but include massages, herbal wraps, salt glow, aromatherapy, East Indian cleaning treatments, Watsu, and acupuncture.

Opened in 1981, Ten Thousand Waves was not always received warmly by locals. The property was once owned by a marijuana grower, who had to dump it in a hurry. Duke Klauck purchased the property with the idea of opening a Japanese-style spa and resort. The grounds were converted to look like a resort in the mountains of Japan, complete with landscaping and bamboo-style construction. The property and services are frequently improved.

Ten Thousand Waves is quite a bit more expensive than most other hot-spring spas. Tub rentals range from $19 to $26 per person, per hour. The communal tub is $13 per person per hour. Spa treatments range from $35 for a 25-minute massage to $300 for a half-day assorted treatment. Hours are Wednesday through Monday from 10 A.M. to 10 P.M., and Tuesday from 4 to 10 P.M. Reservations are highly recommended; call 505-982-9304.

30
Montezuma Hot Springs

General description: A collection of hot springs bubbling out of the side of a hill, feeding a variety of rock and cement tubs. Originally used by the historic Montezuma Castle Resort, the springs are now accessible to the public.

Location: Northern New Mexico, northwest of the town of Las Vegas.

Primitive/developed: Although the springs were once part of the Montezuma Castle Resort, today the tubs lie out in the open, undeveloped.

Montezuma Hot Springs

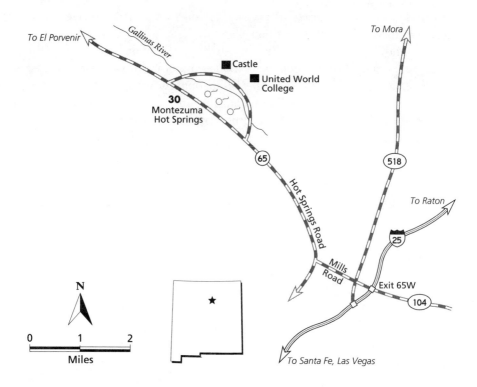

The setting isn't exactly rustic, however, since the springs are located on the side of the road.

Best time of year: Year-round.

Restrictions: Montezuma Hot Springs is owned by the United World College, which allows public access. The owners require bathing suits when using the springs, and the public is not allowed to use the springs between midnight and 5 A.M.

Access: The springs are located immediately off New Mexico Highway 65.

Water temperature: The source is about 138 degrees, The tubs are considerably cooler, ranging from roughly 98 to 112 degrees F.

Nearby attractions: Fort Union National Monument, Santa Fe Trail.

Services: Gas, food, and lodging can be found in Las Vegas, about 6 miles to the southeast.

Camping: Camping is not permitted at Montezuma. Ample camping opportunities are available in the Santa Fe National Forest to the west.

Map: USGS Taos, New Mexico quadrangle (1:100,000 scale).

Finding the spring: From Las Vegas, leave Interstate 25 at exit 65W and cross over to the west side of the highway. Turn right on Business 25 to Mills Avenue, and turn left. Follow Mills for 1.5 miles to Hot Springs Road (which is also NM 65), with signs for Montezuma and the United World College; turn right. Follow Hot Springs Road/NM65 for about 5 miles to the mighty Montezuma Castle on your right. A little farther on you will see signs for the hot springs, immediately off the road on your right. Park along the road and walk to whichever tub you like.

The hot springs: A collection of three groupings of hot springs has been diverted into rather rustic cement and rock pools and tubs along the side of the road in the small community of Montezuma. Originally the Montezuma Castle and several other resorts operated numerous indoor hot-spring pools. Most of the bathhouses are gone now, and the hot springs are out in the open. Pools and tubs range in size and temperature, and with a little experimenting, you can find the perfect soak. Although Montezuma Hot Springs are well known, there are plenty of pools to choose from, and with a little patience, you can always get a tub to yourself. The setting is fantastic, as the springs lie along the Gallinas River adjacent to several historic buildings. Because the owners, the United World College, maintain stringent regulations for using the tubs, they have been kept rather clean, and bathers tend to be orderly. Bathing suits are required, and the pools are closed between midnight and 5 A.M.

The name Montezuma was first applied to the hot springs when a group of soldiers under the command of General Stephen Watts Kearny was marching west during the Mexican War in 1846. In the vicinity of the town of Las Vegas (founded in 1821), the troops ran into the Pecos Indians, who maintained that the famed Mexican leader Montezuma was raised at the springs. Their legend states that he was carried back to Mexico by eagles when he was ready to assume the throne.

Native Americans had been using the springs for centuries, at least since the founding of the Pecos Pueblo in the 800s. Spanish ranchers moved to the area beginning in the early nineteenth century, although the springs saw little development. Prior to, and during the Civil War, a small hospital was erected for ailing soldiers, as was the practice at many hot springs across the country. A small adobe hotel was eventually built at the hot springs in the 1870s, but visitation remained relatively slight.

The Montezuma Castle was constructed by the Santa Fe Railroad Company in 1885 to serve as a grand hotel. The railroad had reached the area in 1878, and bought the property encompassing the hot springs. Originally, the railroad built a small hotel on-site; when it was destroyed by fire, the holding company, the Las Vegas Hot Springs Company, decided to build big. A second, larger hotel containing 240 rooms was constructed. This hotel was also damaged by fire. Finally, the railroad company decided to build a more permanent facility that would become the wonder of the region. The castle was designed by world-renowned architects Burnham and Root, who gave the hotel a kind of medieval, storybook quality. The newer resort also contained several other buildings to take advantage of the nearby hot springs. The hotel was supplied with steam by a massive power plant nearby, which can still be seen. This hotel building was also damaged by fire, and was partially rebuilt in 1886 and renamed the Phoenix. Unfortunately the resort finally closed in 1903.

In 1981, the Armand Hammer Foundation bought the castle for the United World College, but because of neglect the mighty building was structurally unsound. Until recently, the Montezuma Castle was on the National Trust for Historic Preservation's 11 Most Endangered Historic Places List. In 1997, however, local support rallied, and funds have been gathered to repair and restore the castle. Plans call for the college to use the castle as the centerpiece of the campus.

Enjoy the hot springs at Montezuma while you soak in the historic feel of this area. Be sure to pack out all trash and obey all posted regulations.

Fort Union: Just up the interstate from Las Vegas lie the remains of Fort Union, an old cavalry outpost. Established in the 1860s, Fort Union was located along the strategic Old Santa Fe Trail, connecting settlements in New Mexico and the Southwest with the western plains as well as the Midwest. In its heyday, it was the largest fort in the Southwest. Fort Union not only housed several cavalry units but also served as a depot and arsenal for U.S. military operations over a wide region. It became an important supplier to most of the other army posts in Arizona and New Mexico. Today it is the largest collection of adobe ruins in the United States. National Park Service staff have been trying to maintain, stabilize, and repair the adobe buildings since the 1950s. Although efforts have not always been successful, the buildings are in fairly good shape, and give the visitor a feel of what a nineteenth-century military post was like.

From Las Vegas, travel north on Interstate 25 for 21 miles to exit 366 off New Mexico Highway 161. Head west on NM 161 for about 5 miles to the fort.

Taos Area

Serving as a gateway to fantastic hot-spring country, Taos is a destination in itself. Combining pueblos dating back hundreds of years and the modern art scene, Taos is a New Mexico original. There are almost unlimited outdoor activities in the area, from hiking to downhill skiing. Located close to the Rio Grande River, Taos makes a perfect base from which to visit the hot springs of the surrounding countryside. For further information on Taos area hot springs, contact the Carson National Forest at 505-758-6200.

Ponce de Leon Hot Springs.

31

Ponce de Leon Hot Springs

General description: The remains of a onetime thriving hot-spring resort, long abandoned and suffering from neglect and abuse. Today, a natural pool and the remnants of a concrete pool offer bathing opportunities.

Ponce de Leon Hot Springs

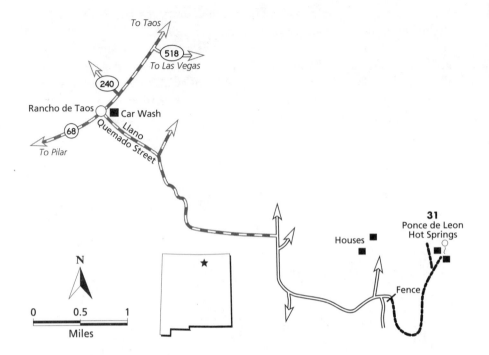

Location: Northern New Mexico, about 8 miles south of Taos.

Primitive/developed: At one time Ponce de Leon was a rather elaborate resort, but all that remains are the ruins of the buildings and pools, and the hot spring itself.

Best time of year: Summer and fall. Roads may be too muddy in winter and spring.

Restrictions: The springs are on private land; be sure to obey all signs. As of this writing, access is still possible. This has changed in the past and may do so again.

Access: A drive of a few miles on a dirt road is required, followed by a hike of about 1 mile.

Water temperature: The hot-spring source is about 100 degrees F; the pools are slightly cooler, averaging 95 to 98 degrees F.

Nearby attractions: Black Rock Hot Springs, Manby Hot Springs, Taos.

Services: Gas, food, and lodging can be found in Taos, about 8 miles to the north.

Camping: No camping facilities are available at the spring, and it is prohibited. Several developed campgrounds are located in the Taos vicinity in the Carson National Forest.

Map: USGS Taos, New Mexico quadrangle (1:100,000 scale).

Finding the spring: From Taos, travel about 4 miles south on New Mexico Highway 68 to Ranchos de Taos. Look for the car wash on your left (east). Turn left onto Llano Quemado Street and follow this road for 0.6 mile to a Y intersection, where you bear right. Continue another 0.4 mile and turn right; the pavement ends here. Continue on this relatively well-maintained dirt road for 1.3 miles to a bend in the road. Park here and follow a dirt road on your right on foot for about 1 mile to where you see the ruins of a large pool and other foundations. Head uphill to the hot spring.

The hot springs: Ponce de Leon was a thriving resort at one time; the immense pool and foundations bear quiet testimony to that. Today, however, all that's left is the spring itself, which forms a small natural pool and then overflows into two cement pools. Depending upon the time of year, the uppermost pool generally makes for the best bath. One of the walls of the pool was bulldozed to discourage swimming at the old resort. Remember that this is not an isolated location, as there are many private residences nearby. Other hot springs and hot wells exist in the area, many of which are used by the households near Ponce de Leon. Be sure to obey all posted signs on the road, as well as at the springs. There have been several occasions when the springs were closed to public access.

32

Ojo Caliente Resort

General description: A busy and thriving resort with a long tradition and lots of history. The resort offers a multitude of mineral spa treatments, ranging from hot water to mud baths.
Location: Northern New Mexico, between Taos and Santa Fe.
Primitive/developed: Developed, but you can still see the sources of the hot springs.
Best time of year: Year-round, although summers can be hot.
Restrictions: Ojo Caliente is a private resort but is open to guests and visitors.
Access: The resort is located immediately off U.S. Highway 285.
Water temperature: There are several sources for the mineral baths, ranging from 109 to 113 degrees F. The pools vary, too, from 85 degrees F in one of the pools to about 106 degrees F in some of the tubs as well as the spa.
Nearby attractions: Taos, Santa Fe, Carson National Forest.

Ojo Caliente Resort.

Services: Gas, food, and lodging can be found in the town of Ojo Caliente, immediately adjacent to the resort. Ojo Caliente Resort also offers lodging, ranging from $52 to $130 per night, depending upon the time of year and accommodations chosen.
Camping: No camping facilities are availble at the resort. Several camp-grounds are located in the nearby Carson National Forest.
Map: New Mexico State Highway Map.

Finding the spring: From Santa Fe, travel 24 miles north on US 84/285 to north of Hernandez, where US 285 splits from US 84. Turn right (north) on US 285 and continue about 18 miles to the town of Ojo Caliente. From Taos, travel 15 miles south on New Mexico Highway 68 to NM 567 in the small community of Pilar. Turn right (west) and follow this road for 18 miles to US 285 (the last part is dirt road). Turn left (south) on US 285 for 11 miles to Ojo Caliente. Once you're in Ojo Caliente, keep an eye out for the resort's sign, and follow a narrow street to the mineral spa.

The hot springs: Rich in history, Ojo Caliente has been enjoyed by countless generations, long before there was a resort here. The resort, however, has been around longer than most in the country. A multitude of baths and treatments

Ojo Caliente Resort

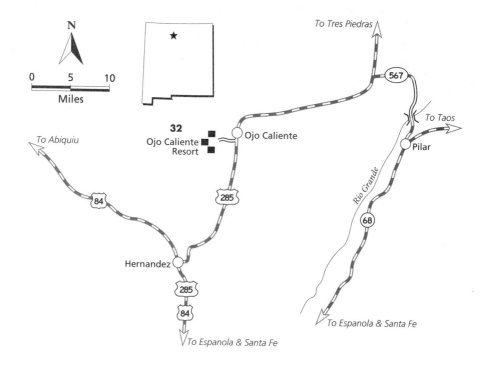

can be found at this unique spot, including several outdoor pools of varying temperatures, individual tubs, massages, wraps, and mud. The high mineral content of the water at Ojo Caliente has been lauded by many who partake of the springs. Iron, arsenic, lithia, and sodium are some of the more prominent, health-inducing minerals, according to some.

Native Americans enjoyed the springs long before seventeenth-century Spanish explorers named them the "hot eye." Pueblo Indians considered the springs sacred, believing them to be an opening to the underworld. Other Native Americans also used the springs, including such distant tribes as the Ute, Comanche, and Navajo. Interestingly, tradition states that the springs were a sort of neutral ground between these groups, who often fought otherwise.

By the early 1800s, Spanish settlers had carved out a small community in the valley near the hot springs, despite continued raids by the Ute and Comanche. The village became known as Ojo Caliente and gained fame the world over. In the 1860s, the hot springs were developed into a resort and, beginning in 1881, could be reached from the Denver and Rio Grande

Railroad and a 10-mile stage ride. During this period, many of the springs were dug out considerably, providing additional bathing opportunities. In 1917, a large hotel was constructed, which still stands. In 1932, the Mauro family acquired the resort, and it remains in the family.

The baths are open between 8 A.M. and 9 P.M. Sunday through Thursday, and until 10 P.M. on Friday and Saturday. Be sure to call 800-222-9162 for further information and reservations.

Rio Grande Gorge

The Rio Grande Gorge, which runs 90 miles north to south through the northern part of the state, proved an impediment to travel for centuries. It wasn't until the late nineteenth century that major transportation routes were built across it. Following the completion of bridges in the early twentieth century, the thriving community of Taos was finally connected to the Denver and Rio Grande Railroad. Interestingly, two of these bridges were constructed close to the first two hot springs described below. Undoubtedly the springs were part of the plans for the area's development. Unfortunately (or fortunately), there was never any lasting development of either of the springs, due to their rugged location, as well as their isolation.

The Rio Grande provides a variety of recreation opportunities, not the least of which is fishing. Be sure to visit these springs during the late summer or early fall. Other times of year are more hazardous and less fulfilling. Roads can be impassable in wet weather, and water levels in the river can be dangerously high. Black Rock Hot Springs, for example, will be totally submerged during high runoff periods.

33

Black Rock Hot Springs

General description: A small grouping of hot springs that forms a small pool alongside the Rio Grande, open only when the river is low.

Location: Northern New Mexico, along the upper reaches of the Rio Grande, west of the small town of Arroyo Hondo, about 15 miles north of Taos.

Primitive/developed: Primitive. The only improvement has been the continual reconstruction of the rock pool that holds the hot-spring water. In the springtime these pools are generally washed out.

Best time of year: Late summer and early fall. Winter is too cold.

Restrictions: None.

Access: The springs are located at the end of a fairly well-maintained dirt road and a 0.25-mile hike. The roads can be impassable in wet weather.

Water temperature: The source is about 106 degrees F. The pools get cooler as the hot-spring water mixes with river water. During the summer, the pools are generally around 98 degrees F.

Nearby attractions: Manby Hot Springs, Taos.

Black Rock Hot Springs

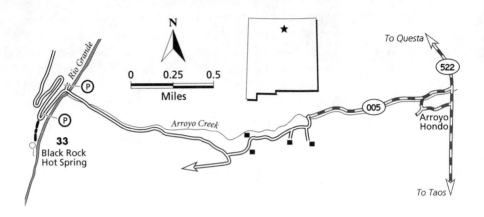

Services: Gas, food, and lodging can be found in Taos, about 15 miles away. Arroyo Hondo offers a small store and lounge.
Camping: No camping facilities are available in the area. There are several campgrounds in the Carson National Forest to the east.
Map: USGS Arroyo Hondo, New Mexico quadrangle (1:24,000 scale).

Finding the spring: From Taos travel north on New Mexico Highway 522 for 11 miles to the small town of Arroyo Hondo. Look for County Road 005 on your left (west) just north of Herb's Lounge and Mini Mart. Travel west on CR 005 for 0.8 mile, where the pavement ends and the road crosses a small bridge. Stay on the main dirt road as it curves uphill, traveling for another 0.7 mile, where you bear right on the main road (the left goes toward houses). Continue for another mile as the road follows the cliffside above Arroyo Creek. Stay right, cross a small bridge, and continue until you reach the Rio Grande. Cross the river on a large steel bridge and turn left on the other side. Follow this dirt road along the Rio Grande for 0.3 mile to a parking area above the river, immediately below where the road makes a hairpin turn. Park here if there's room and follow a fairly well-defined trail upstream for about a quarter of a mile. The hot springs will be identifiable by the small pools on the side of the river, but they're visible only when you're right on top of them.

The hot springs: Located along the spectacular canyon of the Rio Grande, Black Rock Hot Springs is a fun place to visit. Black Rock consists of a small collection of hot springs bubbling into the Rio Grande, which volunteers have captured into one rather large soaking pool. Depending upon river level, the pool can be quite deep (4 feet at times). During the winter, and especially during spring runoff, the hot-spring water will be completely inundated by cold river water and impossible to locate. The pool frequently gets washed out, too. The roads may be too difficult during the wet winter and spring months. Black Rock is fairly well known and easy to reach, so don't expect to have it to yourself. Be sure to practice good hot-spring etiquette when visiting.

In addition to the hot-spring soaking, there are plenty of fishing opportunities in the Rio Grande and in Arroyo Creek, which feeds into the larger river.

34

Manby Hot Springs

General description: A fabulous grouping of hot springs bubbling into several rock-lined pools alongside the Rio Grande. The springs originally were part of a stagecoach stop and mineral bath resort.

Location: Northern New Mexico, along the upper Rio Grande, about 12 miles north of Taos.

Primitive/developed: Although the springs were at one time part of a mineral bath resort, only ruins and makeshift rock tubs remain.

Best time of year: Summer and early fall. Roads may be too muddy in winter and spring, and the pools may be washed out by high water levels.

Restrictions: None.

Access: A 4-mile drive on a dirt road is required, followed by a 1-mile hike. The road may be impassable in wet weather.

Water temperature: The source is about 100 degrees F. The tubs are considerably cooler, particularly when mixed with river water.

Nearby attractions: Black Rock Hot Springs, Taos.

Services: Gas, food, and lodging can be found in Taos, about 12 miles to the south.

Camping: No developed camping facilities are available at the spring, although there are no restrictions against camping nearby. Several developed campgrounds are located in the Taos vicinity in the Carson National Forest.

Manby Hot Springs

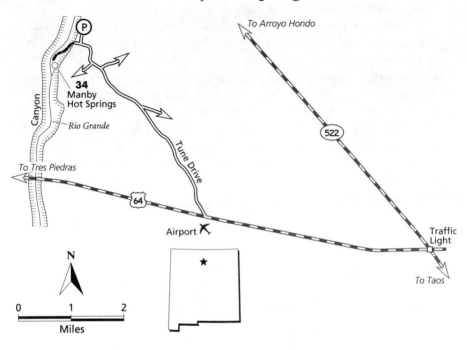

Map: USGS Arroyo Hondo, New Mexico quadrangle (1:24,000 scale).

Finding the spring: From Taos, travel 4 miles north on New Mexico Highway 522 to a blinking light at the intersection with U.S. Highway 64. Turn (left) west and drive about 4 miles to Tune Drive on your right (north). Tune Drive is a graded dirt road, about a third of a mile past the large airport on your left. Take Tune Drive for about 2.8 miles, where you bear left at a Y intersection. Follow signs for Manby Hot Springs. Bear left at another Y intersection, and continue 1.7 miles on this lesser-maintained dirt road to a broad parking area overlooking the Rio Grande canyon. Park here and find a trail on the left (downstream) side of the parking area. Follow this trail as it descends to the river for about half a mile. You will see the hot springs at the end of the trail at the river.

The hot springs: Also known as Stagecoach Hot Springs, Manby is a fantastic place to visit. Consisting of several hot-spring sources, Manby at one time was the location of a raucous resort, complete with a bar, lodge, and, according to some, prostitutes.

As with all other hot springs in the state, Manby was first used and enjoyed by Native Americans. Although Spanish explorers were known to have visited the springs, it wasn't until the late nineteenth century that Euro-Americans began to exploit the location. In the 1890s, two entrepreneurs from nearby Taos decided to build a road that would connect their community with the Denver and Rio Grande Railroad at Tres Piedras. They constructed a toll road across the Rio Grande canyon and a bridge just downstream of the hot springs. The road had to be cut into switchbacks on both banks of the gorge. A stage line traversed the route that stopped at the springs for years immediately prior to the rise of the automobile. In 1906, Arthur Manby acquired property that encompassed the hot springs and decided to put them to good use. He built the large stone bathhouse you see today, with the entrance a full story over the hot water. Guests would take a small staircase down into the hot-water bath. The bathhouse never became all that popular, however, and Manby was unable to turn a profit. He was found dead in his Taos home in 1929, decapitated. Local legend states that Manby's ghost

Manby Hot Springs

roams the area. Following Manby's death, various other owners attempted to make a profit out of the hot springs and its resort.

You can still see the ruins of the various buildings that made up the original resort. The most well-defined ruin is that of the stage station itself. The main bathing opportunity consists of a large rock-lined tub at the edge of the river, several feet deep and several feet wide. This pool's temperature is about 98 degrees F. It does, however, get washed out periodically. A slightly warmer bath lies at the foot of the stagecoach station, provided that it is not washed out, too. This is a great location, with the mighty Rio Grande in the background and the old stage road visible on the opposite bank. Although a well-known spring, you can still find relative seclusion here during the week.

Jemez Indian Reservation and Zia Indian Reservation

Like other Puebloan peoples, those living in the Jemez Canyon were targets of the Spanish people's attempts to establish missions. The Jemez Pueblo was established during this time, and served as a defensive bulwark against the Spanish. The Jemez people fiercely opposed the intervention of the Spanish, and fought them off for over four years. They eventually succumbed to the power of the Spanish. The same people continue to live in the area today, on the Jemez and Zia Pueblo Reservations. Many of their original traditions are still in place.

For information on visiting, contact the Governor of the Pueblo at 505-834-7359.

35

San Ysidro Warm Springs

General description: A collection of several warm springs located alongside a highway near the Jemez Indian Reservation.

Location: Northern New Mexico, west of the town of San Ysidro.

Primitive/developed: Primitive. The springs have not been altered in any way.

Best time of year: Year-round, although summers can be hot.

Restrictions: The land is used for cattle ranching, and there are currently no restrictions. Be sure to obey all signs as they may appear.

Access: The springs are located immediately off New Mexico Highway 44.

Water temperature: The warm springs range in temperature, but average 85 degrees F.

Nearby attractions: Jemez Springs.

Services: Gas, food, and lodging can be found in the town of Bernalillo, about 27 miles to the southeast .

Camping: Camping is prohibited at the warm springs. Several campgrounds are located in the Santa Fe National Forest.

Map: USGS San Ysidro, New Mexico quadrangle (1:24,000 scale).

Finding the spring: From Bernalillo on Interstate 25, head west on NM 44 for 24 miles to the town of San Ysidro. From Jemez Springs, follow NM 4 for about 20 miles to San Ysidro. From San Ysidro at the intersection of NM 4 and 44, go west on NM 44 for about 3.5 miles and look for a place to pull off

San Ysidro Warm Springs
San Ysidro Hot Springs

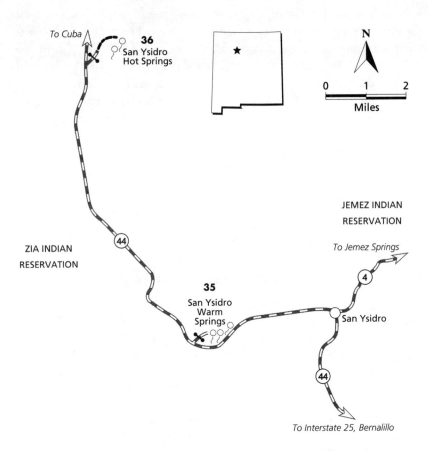

the highway. The warm springs are on your right (north side of the highway), immediately on the other side of a fence. To reach the springs, you must climb over the barbed-wire fence. The springs are spread out over an area of about 0.8 mile.

The hot springs: San Ysidro Warm Springs consists of a collection of small seeps of warm water on the north side of NM 44. The springs are not currently used, except to provide feed for cattle. The minerals in the warm spring water reflect different colors that catch your eye as you are driving along the highway. There are no bathing opportunities at the warm springs, but they make an interesting stop. Be sure to obey all signs as they appear.

36
San Ysidro Hot Springs

General description: A collection of several hot springs located alongside a highway on the Zia Indian Reservation. They are currently closed to the public

Location: Northern New Mexico, 12 miles west of the town of San Ysidro.

Primitive/developed: Primitive. At one time a small resort existed at the springs, but it is now in ruins.

Best time of year: Year-round, although summers can be hot.

Restrictions: As of winter 2000 the springs were off-limits to the public by order of the Zia Indian Reservation. It is hoped this ban will be lifted someday.

Access: The springs are located immediately off New Mexico Highway 44.

Water temperature: The springs range in temperature, but average in the high 80 degrees F.

Nearby attractions: Jemez Springs.

Services: Gas, food, and lodging can be found in the town of Bernalillo, about 37 miles to the southeast. More limited services can be found in Cuba, about 28 miles to the north.

Camping: Camping is prohibited at the springs. Several campgrounds are located in the nearby Santa Fe National Forest.

Map: USGS San Ysidro, New Mexico quadrangle (1:24,000 scale).

Finding the spring: From Bernalillo on Interstate 25, head west on NM 44 for 24 miles to the town of San Ysidro. From Jemez Springs, follow NM 4 for about 20 miles to San Ysidro. From San Ysidro at the intersection of NM 4 and 44, go west on NM 44 for about 12 miles, then look for a place to pull off the highway on your right. The hot springs are on your right (north side of the highway), on the other side of a fence. You can see the foundations of some of the buildings at the end of a small dirt road on the other side of the fence. Unfortunately, the springs are currently closed to the public.

The hot springs: San Ysidro Hot Springs consists of more than 40 springs bubbling up on both sides of the Rio Salado, immediately off NM 44. Several medium-sized pools exist along the banks of the Rio Salado, which were at one time bolstered for bathing purposes. There are also numerous craters in the area, some measuring as wide as 20 feet across. At one time a small resort existed at the springs, complete with at least one structure. Currently, however, the Zia Indian Reservation has restricted public access to the springs, and they are used only by cattle. Obey all signs and do not cross the fence until the ban has been lifted.

FOR FURTHER READING

Back, William, Edward R. Landa, and Lisa Meeks. "Bottled Water, Spas, and Early Years of Water Chemistry," *Ground Water,* Volume 33 (July–August 1995): 605–614.

Kupel, Douglas E. "Taking a Bath: Civic Improvement in Clifton." *The Journal of Arizona History*, Volume 37 (Autumn 1996): 269–282.

Mariner, R. H. T. S. Presser, and W. C. Evans. "Chemical, Isotopic, and Gas Compositions of Selected Thermal Springs in Arizona, New Mexico, and Utah." *Open-File Report 77-654.* U.S. Geological Survey, 1977.

Waring, Gerald A. "Thermal Springs of the United States and Other Countries of the World—A Summary." *Geological Society Professional Paper 492.* U.S. Geological Survey, 1965.

APPENDIX: FOR MORE INFORMATION

USDA Forest Service

Carson National Forest (Black Rock Hot Springs, Manby Hot Springs, Ponce de Leon Hot Springs)
505-758-6200

Gila Wilderness Ranger District (Melanie Hot Springs, Middlefork Hot Springs, Jordan Hot Springs, The Meadows Warm Springs)
505-536-2250

Glenwood Ranger Station (Bubbles Hot Springs, San Francisco Hot Springs)
505-539-2481

Luna Ranger District (Frisco Box Hot Springs)
505-533-6232

Silver City Ranger District (Turkey Creek Hot Springs)
505-538-2771

Santa Fe National Forest
Jemez Ranger District
505-829-3535

Private Hot Springs

Artesian Bathhouse and RV Park
312 Marr
Truth or Consequences, NM 87901
505-894-2684

Charles Motel and Bathhouse
601 Broadway
Truth or Consequences, NM
505-894-7154

Faywood Hot Springs
505-536-9663
faywood@faywood.com

Firewater Lodge
309 Broadway
Truth or Consequences, NM 87901
505-894-3405

Gila Hot Springs Vacation Center (Gila Hot Springs, Wildwood Hot Springs)
505-536-9551

Gila Hot Springs RV Park
505-536-9340

Hot Springs Soaking Pools (Hay-Yo-Kay)
300 Austin
Truth or Consequences, NM 87901
505-894-2228

Indian Springs
218 Austin
Truth or Consequences, NM 87901
505-894-2018

Jemez Springs Bathhouse
P.O. Box 112 - 062 State Highway 4
Jemez Springs, NM 87025
505-829-3303
www.jemez.com/baths

Marshall Hot Springs
311 Marr
Truth or Consequences, NM 87901
505-894-9286

Ojo Caliente Resort
P.O. Box 68
Ojo Caliente, NM 87549
800-222-9162
www.ojocalientespa.com

Radium Springs Resort
P.O. Box 35
Radium Springs, NM 88054

Riverbend Hot Springs
505-894-6183
www.riolink,com/~rivrbnd or e-mail:
rivrbnd@riolink.com

Ten Thousand Waves
P.O. Box 10200
Santa Fe, NM 87504
505-992-5025 Information
505-982-9304 Reservations

INDEX

ABOUT THE AUTHOR

Matt Bischoff is a historian by trade. He greatly enjoys the wide-open spaces and spectacular scenery of the Southwest. Matt grew up in the West and has lived in California, Nevada, and Arizona. He now makes his home in Tucson.

Hot springs have always fascinated him, and seeking out new ones is one of his favorite pastimes. He has explored the Southwest extensively for this book, and for his job, and feels that the hot springs presented here are some of the best in New Mexico.

Matt is the author of *Touring California and Nevada Hot Springs,* and *Touring Arizona Hot Springs,* both published by The Globe Pequot Press.